LONDON TRANSPORT

BUSES & COACHES

1946

LONDON TRANSPORT

BUSES & COACHES

1946

Including a supplement of
photographs covering the years
1939-45 and 1948-55

John A.S. Hambley

Published in 1996 by
IMAGES

in conjunction with
JOHN A. S. HAMBLEY
7 Linden Road,
Dunstable,
Beds. LU5 4NZ

Additional text and research by David A. Ruddom

British Library Cataloguing in Publication Data
A catalogue record for this book is available from the British Library

ISBN 1 897817 82 7

Front cover photograph:

LT29 was to be eventually withdrawn from service in 1947 but prior to its move to Hammersmith garage, where it finally served, it is seen operating from Leyton crossing London Bridge on Route 35 as it makes its way to Clapham Common. The history of this LT started in January 1930 while Route 35 can be traced back to the service introduced in 1906 by the Great Eastern London Motor Omnibus Company between Leyton and Elephant & Castle. This went via Bethnal Green while the 1946 version was via Dalston. Nowadays only the section south of Shoreditch remains. (S.A.Newman)

Back cover photograph:

This broadside view of Weymann, metal framed, twenty seat, front entrance bodied C92 shows the provision made for a route number stencil on the offside of this later batch of Leyland Cubs. The emergency door provided on the offside is also clearly shown. The general appearance of the bus suggests it will need some attention in the near future. On its return from loan to W.T.Edwards of Lydbrook the bus spent a couple of months in store and was then allocated to Hornchurch garage for use chiefly on Routes 238 and 252, its running number 88 indicating its use here on the latter. (Lens of Sutton)

Designed and produced by Images (Publishing) Malvern Ltd.
Printed and bound in Great Britain.

The well photographed ST141, here devoid of any advertising, is seen in Watford High Street just south of The Pond arriving from Chesham on the 336 route on 9th July. With a car parked beside the kerb a little further along the road and the refurbishment to the American Sportswear & Millinery store, an air of post war rehabilitation is apparent which belies the years of austerity which were still to be endured. (A.B.Cross)

Acknowledgements

Without the continued kindness and generosity of many individuals and organisations this series of books could not be produced. For the photographs used within the pages of this volume the author wishes to thank: Norman Anscomb, James H.Aston, R.K.Blencowe, Bob Burrell, C.Carter, Alan B.Cross, The Docklands Museum, John Gascoine, J.C.Gillham, Peter Gomm, The Greater London Record Office, W.J.Haynes, Roger Holmes, Laurie Housden, The Illustrated London News, Fred W.Ivey, D.A.Jones, David Jones, D.W.K.Jones, John Lines, Sheila Taylor of The London Transport Museum, John H.Meredith, A.Mortimer, The Museum of London, K.A.V.Newley, The Omnibus Society, Mrs Joyce Osmond (widow of the late Geoff F.Ashwell), R.A.O'Sullivan, A.D.Packer, John H.Price, D.Purcell, Norman Rayfield, Michael Rooum, Lyndon Rowe, David A.Ruddom, John Smith of Lens of Sutton, John G.S.Smith, Brian Speller, Ron Wellings, Frank Willis and Antony M.Wright.

The factual information on which the picture captions are based has come from published sources and many individuals. The publications of The PSV Circle, The London Historical Research Group of The Omnibus Society and The London Omnibus Traction Society have especially been of great assistance. On a personal note, David Ruddom must be singled out for a special thank you for all his helpfulness, hard work and patience shown to me in the early production stages of the book. My wife Iris and David's wife Enid have kept us supplied with refreshment and shown great patience and forbearance in our long hours of deliberation. John G.S.Smith has also freely given invaluable help and assistance. Thank you.

Publisher's Note

A word of explanation is needed regarding the content of this volume. Genuine photographs of the 1946 year are quite difficult to find. Film was not too readily available and the number of enthusiasts and opportunities for photography were still rather limited. It was not possible therefore to find the usual number of images for this book. However, since publishing the first of the series, which was the 1949 book in 1991, other photographs have come to light which would have merited inclusion in previous volumes had they been to hand at the time. So I have decided to use the available space to include a selection of these pictures as a supplement to this volume which I hope readers will find acceptable.

The number of photographs used within this series of books for which it has not been possible to identify their origin has slowly diminished with each new title. Research has not provided any clues to the few such pictures contained in these pages but if this can be rectified in later volumes I shall be pleased to do so on receipt of the information and I offer apologies to anyone to whom appreciation may therefore be lacking at present. Further photographer's work appears for the first time in this book and historians, enthusiasts and followers of this very interesting subject will be most grateful to them for allowing their pictures to be published.

Please do get in contact if you have any black and white prints or negatives which could possibly be used in the years still to be covered.

Introduction

During 1946 great efforts were made towards restoring road passenger services to their pre-war levels in the face of great difficulties. This was made possible by a number of factors which, taken as a whole, greatly enhanced the appearance of the fleet in general. Normal working had resumed at Chiswick Works which during the war years had been used for producing parts for the Halifax bombers which were assembled at the unfinished tube depot at Aldenham and completed at Leavesden by London Aircraft Production, a group of London firms co-ordinated by the LPTB. All traces of this activity had now disappeared allowing this huge workshop to once more concentrate on the repair and overhaul of buses and coaches. Outside help with renovating and rebuilding a number of different types of vehicles was implemented on a large scale with nearly 250 buses and coaches being dealt with and which were returned to service during the year. The return of loaned vehicles from the US Army, ENSA, provincial operators and the emergency services aided the operation of services. The last influx of additional vehicles was provided by the delivery of new vehicles from no fewer than four different chassis manufacturers. While this did not help the normal LPTB policy of standardisation, it was a case of obtaining whatever vehicles were available. Altogether 304 new vehicles were delivered to the Board while at the same time only 28 were actually withdrawn from service. This enabled a modest number of changes to be made to the network.

Route changes during 1946 were limited and can be generalised by saying that while the Central Area concentrated on restoring frequencies and levels of service at evenings and weekends, the Country Area indulged in some expansion. This was most notable in the restoration of Green Line coach services but also in the provision of some services to previously unserved areas. Examples of this can be found early in the year in the Dartford area where new route 491 served Chastilian Road at Dartford and also with the introduction of route 419 at Epsom and 432 between Guildford and Great Bookham. Changes in the northern area did not occur until the summer programme when a revision in Watford removed the trunk 321 route from Queens Road and introduced the 334 and 334A. The 310A was re-routed to follow the 310 along the Great Cambridge Road and it was many years before the 310A number returned to Ponders End and the Hertford Road and then only as a predatory red bus service by London Northern.

The most notable return to peacetime standards was the resumption of the Green Line services made possible by the Government who announced that Regional Traffic Commissioners would be in a position to consider applications from express coach operators in the early months of the year. Vehicles were available and it was no problem to start a programme of resumption which commenced with two routes on the 6th February. The opportunity was taken to introduce a new network of services which reflected perceived passenger needs rather than replicate the pre-1939 scene. The new pattern was largely to embrace cross-London services although there were exceptions and the routes were given numbers starting at 701. Interestingly, one cross country service, to be numbered 719, from Windsor to Luton via Watford and St.Albans was planned but never appeared.

As already stated, the Central Area concentrated on improving existing services and actual changes to the network were limited. Some of the routes introduced to meet wartime needs disappeared. Examples were the 231 from Waltham Abbey to Epping Town, the section to the Wake Arms being covered by a daily extension to 242 and the withdrawal of the extension of route 2 beyond Golders Green to Arnos Grove. This latter service was replaced by local route 251A between North Finchley and Arnos Grove.

Another sign of the changed conditions was the restoration of three conducted coach tours and special services to major sporting events.

The pre-war fleet was now another year past its expiry date thereby proving more and more difficult to keep in good working order. The promised deliveries of the post-war RT class which should have started during the year never materialised. There was still a shortage of operating staff due mainly to more attractive wages being offered to industrial workers. Skilled labour at the garages and Chiswick Works was still in short supply but nevertheless the general public were enjoying a steadily improving service.

Although no new operational garages were opened during the year, two older establishments were brought back into use with the re-introduction of Green Line services. These were Tunbridge Wells (TW), which had been used as an ambulance station for some years and Romford, London Road (RE) which had laid idle for a similar period.

On the vehicle front new deliveries were made up of the Daimler chassised vehicles, the D class, the last of which were delivered being 140 in total. The residue of the Guy Arab class (G), 19 in total, the complete batch of the new Leyland post-war Titan PD1 model numbered in the STD class which totalled 65. The 20 post-war STL buses were delivered, the first three being in red livery although the entire batch were for use in the Country Area. Single deck buses were also added in the shape of a further 50 members of the T class given fleet numbers T719 to T768 and the first ten of some Leyland Tiger PS1s which were numbered into a new TD class, resurrecting a pre-war classification. The small number of withdrawals consisted of 1C, 5LTs, 5Qs, the prototype RT1, 14 members of the ST class and 2Ts.

London Transport, never short of new ideas, returned rebuilt RT97 to service as a Pay As You Board bus operating from Kingston garage where it joined STL2284 which was still in use using the idea of a seated conductor. This arrangement did not prove successful as it considerably slowed down operation and after a spell in the Central Area the STL moved on to the Country Area and the RT to Green Line work from Romford, the experiment being abandoned before the year ended.

Finally, in recognition of the valiant work carried out by London Transport and its staff during the Second World War, RT4 and RT39 had the honour of representing the Board in the mechanised column of the Victory Parade through central London in the second week of June. In addition a number of employees formed a squad in the march past.

On 22nd May the 216 route terminal stand in Kingston was moved from the overcrowded Bus Station to the lay-by adjoining the railway station in Wood Street. There appears to be little protection for the passengers queuing for the 418 route either from the rain or from a "scooter" that might skid on the wet surface. The driver presumably of LT1155 makes his way to his bus where passengers have availed themselves of a seat to escape the hostile weather conditions. Originally built with a seating capacity of 35 this was altered to 33 peripheral seats with standing for 20 in July 1942 and this arrangement was to remain until the vehicle was withdrawn from service in June 1949. The bus was then disposed of to Daniels of Rainham who at the time were receiving most of LT's obsolete fleet. (Omnibus Society)

Photographed at Uxbridge Station, soon after entering service with LPTB Weymann bodied T727 works Route 223. This batch of buses were the first post-war single deckers to be purchased and were fitted with 7.7litre engines, crash gearboxes and triple-servo brakes. There were fifty in total and they carried fleet numbers T719 to T768 with registration numbers HGF809 to HGF858 and bodies numbered 1155 to 1204 respectively. All through their working life in London the bodies stayed on the chassis to which they were first mounted. This is one of the examples carrying chrome windscreen surrounds but in due course these were painted red.

Still holding on to its white painted fender, which looks to be in need of some attention, C66 stands beside Chelsham garage dressed for use on Route 465 between Holland and Edenbridge (Star) as CM19. The white strip carried at the rear and which continued just around the offside corner is also still in place from the blackout years. The almost camouflaged bollard in the bottom right of the picture invites an unwary driver to collide with it. (Omnibus Society)

The "Courtesy Aids Service" slogan proclaimed by the sticker adjacent to the platform of ST141 was part of a special campaign launched by management and unions on 19th March to try to improve the poor level to which staff/passenger relations had sunk. Whilst aimed primarily at staff the position of the poster shows that the public needed to play their part as well in the difficult times. The bus still carries a petrol engine as shown by the Autovac on the bulkhead but in December 1949 this would disappear when the bus was re-engined with a diesel powered example. (G.F.Ashwell)

Viewers can judge for themselves whether Q145's appearance is enhanced or demeaned by the new livery it received later when comparing this print with that of the same vehicle which appears on page 61 of the 1951 book of this series. The visual impact is completely changed by the different paint scheme and personally I admit I like this combination of red and white rather more than the later overall red with cream relief bands. Here the bus is seen at the Cricklewood Broadway stand of the short 226 route to Golders Green. (R.F.Mack)

In the early summer STL2687 still has not been marred with any advertising, although it first entered service in January. Twenty of these handsome provincial style metal framed Weymann bodied AEC Regent Mark IIs were licenced to be purchased for LPTB requirements by the Ministry of War Transport. The brown roof colour is carried slightly down the front upper deck corner pillars. The bus is standing at an incredibly peaceful Uxbridge Station before setting out on the long 321 route to Park Square at Luton. (Michael Rooum)

Ex-T392 wears khaki livery while resting at the Buchholz Barracks in Hanover earlier in the year than in the picture which appears later in this book. The Dodson body is one of only two such make ever carried by members of the T class, the other being numbered T391 which continued in London Transport service through to 1949. Both had been acquired from Bucks Expresses (Watford) Ltd. in February 1932 when they carried an attractive chocolate colour scheme. The higher numbered of the pair, which was disposed of to the War Department for the Control Commission, Germany in May 1945, is here being used as transport for the BAOR Combined Services Football XI. It had the military identification M6073466 as can be seen along the top of the engine cover. (J.H.Price)

The only one of the elegant TF private hire coaches to survive the war was TF9. It is pictured still basically in the condition and colour scheme in which it first entered service in April 1939. Garage and running plate holders together with brackets for a slip board on the sliding door are later additions. The front wheel disc is now finished in the same colour as the main part of the bodywork and it temporarily lacks its rear wheel disc. The coach is in the vicinity of St.Pauls Cathedral on a "Seeing London Tour". A very limited programme of three tours had been introduced on 11th June and this illustrates the morning tour of Westminster and the City. (G.F.Ashwell)

All the 2RT2 class vehicles found themselves operating from the two Putney garages by 1946, the first full year since the cessation of World War II hostilities. RT16, having lost its rear offside wheel disc, operates as AF3 on route 30 and makes its way to Roehampton, the southern terminus of the route. Originally entering service on 2nd January 1940, one of the first batch of fifteen RTs to do so, the bus is now over six years old and looks in need of attention at Chiswick. Upon its post-war overhaul it would lose this livery for the latest style which removed the light relief to the lower saloon window surrounds.

A long way from its original operating territory of the 109, later 227, route between Eltham, Chislehurst and Penge, ex-Tilling T312 now finds itself at Uxbridge Underground Station working route 222 to Hounslow Central Underground Station. Only two of these 1932 petrol engined buses appear to have strayed to Uxbridge garage during their operating lives, the other being T307. Once removed from their Bromley home members of the type, which numbered twelve, had the distinction of operating as far afield as Dalston, Enfield, Hornchurch, Hounslow, Kingston, Leyton and Tottenham. The Tilling built body style always looked antique, even in its early days. (W.J.Haynes)

LT104 first entered service in October 1930 from Leyton garage and sixteen years on looks in remarkably good condition while picking up passengers outside the National Gallery on route 134 working from Potters Bar garage. However, looks can be deceptive since in October 1947 the chassis would be exchanged with that from LT41 and the latter scrapped. The body number 11177 of LT2 type with its different chassis then soldiered on until withdrawn from service, still at Potters Bar garage, in June 1949. The wording of the Wrigley's advertisement is intriguing, "chew for health" is debatable but courage and fortitude are incomprehensible, unless it hides your chattering teeth! (J.H.Price collection)

STL1263 with STL1227 close behind are working duties W8 and W9 respectively on Route 60 and they are parked between peaks on Victoria Embankment having finished their morning duties at Charing Cross. STL1263 carries the body originally fitted to DST1. DST1 to DST3 were bought new by the LGOC in 1931, being Daimler CH6 chassis fitted with sleeve valve petrol engines but introducing the first pre-selective gearboxes and fluid flywheels to the fleet. All three were fitted with LGOC built ST type bodies. Due to the poor performance derived from the engines they were all withdrawn from service in 1935/36 and the bodies transferred to a special batch of STL chassis with a wheelbase of 15'6½", as against the normal for the class which was 16' and over. All three continued in service carrying the bodies which were given the code STL10 until withdrawn from service in 1949/50. STL1227 behind is and always was a 2/9STL11, the body being a normal Chiswick product of 1936. (P.Gomm collection)

Pictured at the Golders Green terminus of Route 28, STL155 operating from Middle Row garage appears to have a broken running number holder which has resulted in the plate being jammed in with the garage one. Passengers have availed themselves of a seat within the bus away from the wintry elements indicating that it will soon be departing for Wandsworth. This STL with its LGOC built body numbered 13499 was one of those which received the short lived livery of overall red with two cream bands on its overhaul in December 1945. The modern approach never suited these vehicles which looked much happier in the LGOC red and broken white. (D.A.Ruddom collection)

STD149 entered service in November operating from Loughton garage but the opportunity was taken to photograph the bus ready for service beforehand. The batch consisted of sixty five buses numbered STD112 to STD176. A Leyland PD1 chassis of 16'3" wheelbase, 7.4 litre oil engine, single plate clutch and four speed constant mesh gearbox carried a Leyland designed and built 56 seat body with minor London Transport modifications. No rear destination equipment was provided but in later years a route number stencil similar to that fitted here next to the entrance was fixed at the top of the rear platform window. Note that the white blackout spot is still added to the rear. (LT Museum 19630)

The driver doesn't seem to have got the hang of how to set the blinds correctly on somewhat dusty D146. Although the precise location of this picture has not been identified, it makes a change from the Aldgate terminus where most views of these new Green Line Daimlers seem to have been taken. (S.L.Poole)

The new Green Line D class vehicles attracted the attention of many transport photographers as will be evident from a study of the pages of this book. While still in 1946, this is a view taken later in the year when the black on yellow (or amber as some called it) destination blinds had been fitted. D176 stands at Aldgate with chassisless class L3 trolleybus 1440 working from Poplar Depot in the background. (S.A.Newman)

Chelverton Road's RT14 lays over at the Wakefield Road bus station in Richmond before commencing a journey to fit into the mainstream workings of Route 37 which ran between Hounslow Bus Station and Peckham. (L.Housden collection)

A batch of AEC Regals with Weymann bodywork, delivered between April and July, were the latest additions to the T class and represented here by T720. Route 223 buses called into the Bus Station at Uxbridge on their way from Ruislip and this one looks to be about to continue its journey to West Drayton. Parked closely behind the 1946 Weymann bodied example one of the small number of 1932 Tilling bodied Ts allocated to Uxbridge garage at the time illustrates the tremendous variety of vehicle encompassed in the T class. (K.A.V.Newley collection)

This rear end view of bomb blasted LT21 clearly shows some of the measures which had to be taken to keep such damaged vehicles in operational service. This bus had received damage at the Aldwych in 1944 and is still fitted with smaller panes of glass in the rear lower deck platform window and the fourth window of the lower deck saloon, although it should be noted that the enclosed staircase body, number 11670, was received in March 1940. It had already received an oil engine in June 1935 and is therefore unique in being the only 2/12LT3/1. (R.Burrell)

"Inter-station" C111 rests on Eccleston Bridge with the once familiar roof of Victoria railway station as a backdrop. A livery of sky-blue and cream was carried for duties on the service between the major London rail termini. All eight of these Park Royal bodied 20 seat Leyland SKPZ2s delivered in 1936 were loaned to ENSA for varying periods from 1942. By 1946 all had been returned whereupon they were repainted from their temporary livery of khaki and returned to their proper use. However immediately after the war some were allocated to airport services and this Cub is employed on the Channel Islands Airways service between Victoria and Croydon Airport. Happily this vehicle is preserved in its Inter-station form by Alan Cross. (W.J.Haynes)

Almost as if on parade, nine well parked buses could be guarding the building of Chelsham garage. From left to right the first bus is unidentifiable but then we have STL591, STL597, STL577, STL564, STL2480, STL2021, STL590 and C4. Interestingly, all the double deckers first entered service finished in Central Area red livery and STL2480 still carries this colour scheme. In September 1946 however it too succumbed and followed the trend started by STLs564 and 577 in March 1941. C4, a long term resident of the garage, was to receive the newer Country Area paint scheme before being withdrawn from service with the arrival of the new GS class in 1953. (Omnibus Society)

Victoria garage became involved with Route 77 on 12th December 1945 when the part of the Monday to Saturday allocation provided by Chalk Farm was replaced by the newer garage using STL class vehicles. STL1331 with running duty plates GM40 stands empty with its blind set for a run-in to the garage via Vauxhall Bridge Road. The body, number 437, is interesting in that it is one of only twelve STL17 built in the second half of 1941 by the LPTB. Due to the effect of war damage reducing the available float bodies of this class, sanction was sought for the build and given by the Ministry of War Transport. The bodies were built as closely as possible to resemble the large batch of STL16 produced just prior to the outbreak of the war subject to necessary modifications caused by wartime shortages. As this picture clearly shows there were small differences, for example in the plain mudguards, non-opening upper deck front windows, lack of an opening ventilator flap above the driver's windscreen and one less opening set of windows to the lower saloon.

(L.Housden collection)

Tilling bodied STL90 was eventually withdrawn from service in November 1947, although it appears to be in reasonable shape here, having served Londoners for around fourteen years. The body of type STL4 numbered 14067 is basically as it first appeared when it entered service on the 112A between Park Royal and East Dulwich late in February 1933 operating from Catford garage. Of course the livery has changed over the years, London Transport replacing Thomas Tilling, the side lights have been moved from between decks to the more usual position as shown but except for the last lower saloon window being boarded up and a route stencil fitted, no major changes have occurred. The wartime style of blind display, if slightly less informative, is clearer to read than the overcrowded design used when these vehicles were new. (R.H.G.Simpson)

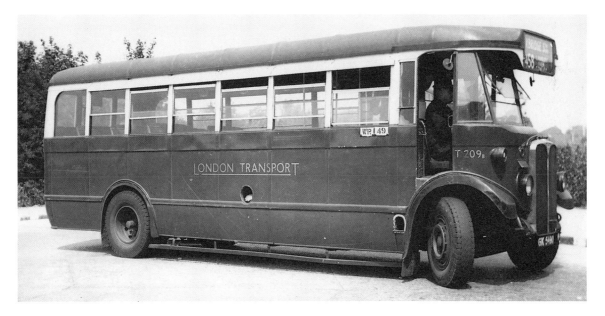

T209b had worn the temporary service fleet number 431W while in use as a staff ambulance from September 1939 through to August 1945. Provision was made for these vehicles to accommodate ten stretchers by the removal of all seating and the enlargement of the rear emergency doorway which involved re-positioning the door pillars and these were never altered afterwards. The vehicles were repainted into standard lorry livery of dark green which included the saloon windows. The bus, now returned to peacetime duties, operates as WR49 on Route 458 at Uxbridge Stn.Und., which is the destination shown. The one piece blind box projects below the canopy in the same position as that originally occupied by the lower Green Line box.

LT75 now carries one of the original fifty 60 seat open staircase bodies with square cab built by the LGOC. The body (No.10326) was originally mounted on the chassis of LT24 but with the overhaul procedure used at Chiswick Works has over the years been mounted on various LT class chassis. Loughton and Leyton garages provided this class of vehicle for the 10A route and this example is operating from the former. It is seen at the Green Man, Leytonstone and before the year is out it would be transferred upon the arrival of the post-war STD class at this garage. (R.Burrell)

Photographed at Epsom racecourse in August, former DA13 is now in use as a showman's living quarters. The bus entered service in 1930 to open up new routes where traffic was expected to be sparse and with only 18 seats operated as an o.m.o. vehicle, a use permitted as long as the vehicles involved did not seat more than 20. The restricted headlamps are masked in an unusual fashion to say the least while a lucky horseshoe, as befits its location, is attached to the radiator grille. (S.A.Newman)

Merton garaged D81 wearing brown livery stands at Clapham Common with Streatham's STL2580 before both buses depart their separate ways for Oxford Circus and Raynes Park respectively. The Duple body, numbered 715, on the Daimler would receive its normal Central Area livery in July 1948. Simplicity is the keyword of the soft drinks advertisement on the side. (D.W.K.Jones)

Ex-GF125 is seen after the war when it was probably owned by Miss P.Solomons who traded as Blue Rambler Motor Coaches of London. It is parked beside a nice little coach belonging to Reece of Chatham on what must have been a fine outing for both parties. The early history of GF125 is that it was new in March 1932 as Edward Hillman's Saloon Coaches of 127/9 Bow Road, London fleet number 112. A Wycombe 26 seat front entrance coach body was mounted on a 168MOT chassis. Hillman's had the largest fleet of this make of chassis in the country and it was in August 1934 that the last vestige of this operator was acquired by the LPTB. JD1981 was given fleet number GF125 and after a short period of operation was withdrawn in 1936. It was stored at the AEC premises at Walthamstow until sold to Dawson, a dealer in South West London in December 1937. By May 1946 it was in the ownership of Miss Solomons. Acquired for preservation in November 1964 it is thought to be the only known survivor of the Hillman fleet.
(N.Anscomb collection)

Parked within the vicinity of Baker Street T577c, with half its operating crew silhouetted inside, takes a breather from operating between the capital and the Surrey town of Reigate some thirty miles to the south. In 1947 this Green Line route was extended through to High Wycombe replacing the 724 route which had worked between Oxford Street and the town nestling at the foot of the Chiltern Hills in Buckinghamshire. (W.J.Haynes)

ST190 closely followed by T412b is seen at the Epsom Racecourse late in the day with intending passengers boarding for the short journey down to Epsom Station. To the right of the picture LPTB's route survey vehicle 305M, a 30cwt. Morris "EA" appears to have been put to use as a radio communications post. The raised gantry was normally used to check clearances on new routes or diversions. Here it appears to support an aerial for this early example of radio control of buses. (J.G.S.Smith collection)

ST and STD class vehicles keep G259 company within the Golders Green bus station. The Massey bodied Guys were the most angular of the utilities and their gingery brown livery with no relief did little to enhance their appearance. Seating for 56 passengers, the recognised standard for the period, is provided and the body of this particular example was numbered 882 by London Transport and 1653 by its builders. (D.W.K.Jones)

Oil engined "Bluebird" type LT999 on route 145 at the Chingford Station stop only has the short run into Epping Forest up Rangers Road to complete before taking its stand outside the Royal Forest Hotel. The bus was to survive until May 1949 in service from Seven Kings garage, who received it in the closing months of 1945 from Plumstead and, as with the majority of vehicles destined to be scrapped at the time, was finally despatched to R.L.Daniels. (A.B.Cross)

On 11th September the somewhat remote Central Area route 206 from Claygate to Imber Court was extended up to Hampton Court Station and the one-man-operated Cs were replaced by crew-operated Ts. This broadside view at the new terminus of the nearside of T756 clearly shows the sliding window arrangement fitted to this batch of 50 Weymann single deck bodies manufactured in 1946. The wheelbase of these 14T12s was 17′6″ while the overall length was 27′4″. Crash gearboxes with single plate clutch delivered the power to the rear wheels from the 7.7litre oil engine fitted. The dented bodywork at the rear suggests the larger buses may have experienced a little difficulty negotiating the route! (L.Housden collection)

This rear view of RT97 clearly shows the orthodox upper deck rear emergency window matched with one provided in the lower saloon. The blind box over the platform was reduced to the size of those used on LTs and STs in order to accommodate the door mechanism beneath but the reason for the reduction in size of the rear box is uncertain. The rearmost nearside lower deck window is a fixed pane and as late as 1946 it was considered appropriate to still include the white disc together with a white leading edge to the platform area, although this latter feature may have served to draw attention to the second step hidden behind the sliding doors. The bus carries blinds ready for its intended use on Kingston's small allocation on Route 65 and it entered service on 2nd January, the day after this photograph was taken. (J.G.S.Smith collection)

Q188 was the only three-axle "Q" type vehicle ever built carrying chassis number 763001 and LPTB body number 16130. It is seen here after sale by the Board. Originally ordered to carry forward the indulgence of experimenting with double deck Green Line coaches, it was delivered in February 1937 being first registered in the following month. It had been intended for use on the Aldgate, Romford and Brentwood Green Line operations but due partly to inadequate performance and trade union opposition it never entered service as a coach, being relegated to bus work in the Hatfield and Hertford area of Country bus operations. Delicensed at the outbreak of war it was never used again in London, being disposed of to Lancashire Motor Traders of Manchester in March 1946. It quickly passed to H.Brown, a local operator of Garelochhead in whose service it is seen with the B of Brown nicely added to the triangular area of the imitation radiator now fitted.

Having been returned from its former use as a public ambulance in March and quickly re-converted for passenger use, green and white liveried T408b now finds its first duty on Central Area route 3 operating out of Norwood garage. This was a move by LPTB starting on 17th June to combat the vehicle shortage and routes 54 and 137 were also the recipients of some of these comfortable coaches. The 9T9 is seen at the Camden Gardens stand in company with an STL, the normal type used on the route which was shared by Chalk Farm and Norwood garages. (W.J.Haynes)

STL85 with Tilling bodywork carries the example married to the chassis in March 1939 upon its fifth overhaul. This combination then remained together until withdrawal from service took place in September 1949 and the vehicle was scrapped by R.L.Daniels. It is seen parked at Bromley North while working on Route 138 to Hayes, Coney Hall. This route had been double-decked on 27th November 1940 and renumbered from its single deck series designation of 232.

(J.G.S.Smith collection)

The post-war batch of sixty-five all-Leyland 4STD3 type began to enter service in October 1946 and by Christmas all were earning their keep. Although being quite a small number they were spread around no fewer than five garages, namely Victoria, Hanwell, Loughton, Potters Bar and Croydon. Those at Potters Bar however only remained there for an extremely short period and open staircase LTs replaced them by 20th November. STD124 arrives at Leytonstone as GM6 on a short working of route 10. In the background LT58 sets out for Epping Town on route 10A while a "Bluebird" LT is about to return to Dagenham Dock via the roads of route 148.

(J.H.Price collection)

Looking in need of attention, Windsor garaged T302 stands at the Uxbridge terminus of route 458 before returning to Slough. This vehicle, once a Green Line coach, first entered service in February 1931 from Romford, London Road (RE) garage, was used as an ambulance during the war years and finished its operational career with London Transport in 1949 as a bus. Nowadays the new Uxbridge garage occupies the land area immediately beyond the parked car. (London Trolleybus Preservation Society)

Originally delivered on 26th October 1939 CR16's first peacetime duties after its enforced storage during much of the war years were in June of the year under review. Its first operational base was Streatham before being transferred to Merton later in the year. It is seen in Liverpool Street, which was the stand used by Route 133 in 1946, the evacuation to Finsbury Circus happening in July 1947. The corner white areas painted on for the blackout when the green liveried bus was operating from Windsor garage have still to be removed.

Looking splendid from the recent attention given it by the Chiswick workforce having spent the previous six-plus years as an ambulance, petrol engined LTC14c now finds work in its originally intended role as a private hire vehicle. It is seen standing within the grounds of Alexandra Palace on some sort of contract duty for the BBC. Through the windows can be seen the extra large fully upholstered seating provided within the Weymann body which closely resembled the Chiswick built 10T10s. In February 1950 the petrol engine fitted from new would be replaced by a diesel example from a scrapped STL. The small panel above the filler cap, similar to the advertisement frames used in recent times, was retained but its original use carrying tour boards was seemingly lost in later years. (D.W.K.Jones)

ST204 was returned to London service to operate from Camberwell garage after its temporary wartime loan to Cumberland Motor Services of Whitehaven. It is seen while in use on the long standing 42 route with destination blind showing Camberwell Grn. (L.Housden collection)

ST772 had been on loan to the Lincolnshire Road Car Company for the period October 1942 to September 1946. The bus, still carrying its livery and Lincolnshire fleet name looks a little dejected as it stands outside the boiler house at Chiswick Works on 30th October. In April of the following year it was scrapped and although the PSV Circle record its final allocation as Croydon it is doubtful if it ever re-entered passenger service in London. (J.C.Gillham)

The ST class vehicles which had been painted blue and cream and specially adapted for use on the Inter-Station service during the war returned to normal duties as the deck and a half Leyland Cubs returned from loan to ENSA during the year covered by this book. This view of the lower deck of ST613 clearly shows the space created for luggage by the removal of eight seats. Note the protective upright bars added to the windows in this area. The picture is also a pleasant reminder for older readers of the interior decor of an ST. (L.Housden collection)

ST164 on the 15th July wearing Inter-Station blue and cream colours is pictured outside Victoria Southern Railway station while engaged on this link service to all the other major railway termini in London. A number of seats have been removed to allow for luggage space and upright safety bars are fitted to the windows forward of the staircase for this purpose. After reconversion and repainting into red livery in June 1947 the bus only saw further use as a trainer until withdrawal from the fleet in May 1949 and eventual despatch to Daniels of Rainham in February 1950 for scrap. (G.F.Ashwell)

Q210c stands in the yard at High Wycombe garage having been transferred there from Hertford during the summer. Route 724 commenced operation on 3rd April between Oxford Circus and this market town nestling in the valley of the River Wye, less well known than its namesake much further west on the main A40 road which runs through the town. All 238 Q type vehicles had extremely short overhang at the rear and this example of a 6Q6 shows this phenomenon well. The coaches used the standard wheelbase rather than the shorter one used by the 5Q5 Central Area buses resulting in an equally short overhang at the front. (W.J.Haynes)

Two of the Guy Arab Mark II buses with Weymann bodywork garaged at Barking are seen parked at the King's Oak, High Beach. G412, the main subject of the photograph, has stablemate G416 keeping it company. These examples of the then 435 strong class carried classification 1/3G11 and LT body numbers 1035 and 1039 respectively. The Weymann bodies always seemed to have a sense of airy spaciousness compared to those by NCME and Massey and they also had the luxury of winding saloon windows. The centrally placed "Pip" winders can just be seen in this view. (W.J.Haynes)

This print is included as it shows the original Hatfield bus garage with STL604 changing crews outside and another two STLs lurking inside the dark interior. The so-called "leaning back" STL, not too common in green, had received Country Area colours in November 1945 and is working the western section of Route 341 between Hatfield and St.Albans for which a "lazy" blind is displayed. (A.B.Cross)

Standing alongside Croydon garage LT1149 is parked nicely on the roadway waiting for further use having worked up the Brighton Road from Purley after its stint on Route 234. Just in view is a newly delivered post-war STD class vehicle primarily intended for Route 115. First entering service in July 1931 the LT originally carried a body with a rear destination blind. Subsequent body changes have resulted in it now carrying the earlier type only fitted for boards at the rear. It was one of those selected to be renovated by Marshalls of Cambridge in 1949 and later in June 1950 its petrol power unit was exchanged for a diesel example. Final withdrawal from service came in March 1952 by which time the bus was a grand old lady. (Michael Rooum)

In murky winter conditions brand new STD160, having only entered service in November, waits departure from Leytonstone on Route 10A. Despite the luxury of a closed-in cab for the driver and a covered platform and staircase for the conductress the crew prefer to chat in the open beside one of the wartime introduced shelters which afforded little protection from the elements. (R.Burrell)

C74b waits within Hertford Bus Station for further use, probably on Route 333, with running plates HG21. Eventually this twenty seater would be exported to Ceylon, being lengthened to seat forty one passengers by the South Western Omnibus Company (Ceylon) Ltd. of Colombo who then re-registered it IC2500. (L.Housden collection)

D139 is seen waiting at Clapham Common for a return journey to Raynes Park. This bus is from the third highbridge batch of this class bodied by Duple, delivery of which commenced in November 1945. 118 was the number used for the replacement of the section of Route 5 between Clapham Common and Mitcham Common on the 18th November 1936 and was operated by LT vehicles from Streatham garage. STL class buses replaced the LTs in December 1939 and Merton garage became involved on 7th January 1942 when the route was extended to Raynes Park and they also used STLs. With the introduction of the D class at AL they first appeared on the route on a Sunday only basis but were allocated on a daily basis from 10th October 1945.

This picture of T702c as it rests on Eccleston Bridge, Victoria, before departing for East Grinstead on duty EG56 is very similar to that shown in the 1948 book of this series of the same vehicle. There are however subtle differences. In this May 1946 view the small "c" after the fleet number is carried denoting that the vehicle is a coach. By 1948 the front offside mudguard has been rebuilt to a hybrid assembly which owes something to the 9T9 variety of coach and the wheel trims have been altered. Most prominent is the style of blind fitted, which in this view is the second post-war type that only existed in May 1946. Still white on black, it has a layout more akin to the black on amber variety which superseded it at the end of the month. (G.F.Ashwell)

G class vehicles took over operation of the 107 and 107A routes, replacing STLs, following on the conversion of route 102 which had started the previous year. G285 with NCME bodywork operates as E11 and is seen arriving at the Arkley Hotel terminus at Barnet during its first full year in service. The bus advertises Daryl F.Zanuck's latest production 'Anna and the King of Siam' with Irene Dunne, Rex Harrison and Linda Darnell. It was a few years yet before the story was retold on the screen in the musical 'The King and I'. (D.W.K.Jones)

When it first entered service in April 1930, PG7726 operated as number 217 in the East Surrey fleet, receiving LPTB fleet number ST1094 in 1935. Bodywork is of Ransomes, Sims and Jefferies manufacture and provided seating for 49 passengers until this was reduced to 48 in 1939. The bus is parked at the Woodford Road stand at Watford Junction waiting to depart on Route 301 to Tring L.T.Garage while further along the road Q99 is working Route 322 to Hemel Hempstead. (J.Gascoine collection)

STL1522 entered service from Hanwell garage in September 1936 as a 3/9STL11 carrying LPTB body number 16876. Upon its first overhaul in May 1938 it re-emerged from Chiswick Works carrying the body 16849 which had previously been mounted on the chassis of STL1531. In February 1944 the bus gained Country Area colours and in this guise works Route 321 to Luton, Park Square. Here it has pulled into the small lay-by at Croxley Green Station for potential custom. It last worked in passenger service from Swanley Junction garage in September 1952, passing to Merton garage as a trainer during the period March 1953 through to October 1954 before being disposed of to W.North of Leeds in March 1955 for scrap. (W.J.Haynes)

Alperton's G73 stands at the Hayes Station terminus with the station buildings in the distance. The Park Royal bodied bus shares the stand with two STLs the further of which wears the new red livery with just two cream bands. The weekday 83 and Sunday 83A had an all-Guy allocation from Alperton and Hanwell although the latter garage's Bristols strayed this way from time to time to provide variety. In 1946 this vehicle still carried wooden slatted seats and the compiler of this caption painfully recalls a ride on such a vehicle from Ealing to Golders Green. Strange how some bus journeys make a lasting impression! (J.Lines collection)

Standing in Cromwell Road just short of Kingston garage, LT1117 arrives at the end of its journey on Route 213 and has its route blind reset ready for the return journey to its home garage. In the last month of 1948 the bus would be despatched to Marshalls of Cambridge for rebuilding.
(J.G.S.Smith collection)

This vehicle was once DA12 in the LGOC fleet, entering service in 1930 and lasting nine years before being withdrawn from service. The chassis is a Dennis Dart fitted with a 6 cylinder petrol engine driving through a single plate clutch and thence through a 4 speed spur gearbox to the rear axle. Bodywork was built by the LGOC and seated 18 and it is worthy of note that three of the original four glass storm louvres are still in place. The history of the vehicle from when it was sold by the LPTB to Arlington Motors of South West London is not known but it is certainly still in evidence when photographed in the post-war era. The purpose of what looks like a large side route board attached to the roof is unclear. (S.A.Newman)

What was once LT1203, new in November 1931, is photographed in August at Aldenham. It had been disposed of to the British Broadcasting Corporation in August 1939 for use as a mobile radio transmitting vehicle. Four six-wheel chassis were built by the LGOC and designated "CC" at this period to which standard LT type bodies were mounted, this example being of the LT5 type. The buses were fitted with six cylinder petrol engines built by Henry Meadows & Sons of Wolverhampton and drove through a single plate clutch and four speed gearbox to the rear axle. In 1932 the engines were exchanged for AEC built units and all four were withdrawn from service in May 1939. (K.A.V.Newley collection)

The interior of a Duple bodied Daimler in April 1946 carrying one of that manufacturer's earlier built bodies with wooden slatted seating and only two opening windows each side to the saloon. Ventilators are provided at the front of the upper deck with numerous advertisers taking advantage of the space permitted. Both the front dome adverts refer to tobacco products with the statutory "Do not spit - penalty £5" notice between them - why was it only £2 on trams?! Moquette seating was substituted for that shown in the period 1948/49. (V.C.Jones)

STL1167 carries body number 15781, the original full fronted STL11 variety used on STF1 and now partly rebuilt with half width cab. It operates as Q3 on Route 59A with blinds set for Camden Town. In the book of this series which covers the year 1948 the bus can be viewed having been rebuilt even further with the elimination of the pronounced front slope although the provision of the numerous opening windows is retained. (W.J.Haynes)

Originally built in 1931 as an experimental single deck bus by the LGOC and bodied for 29 passengers, ex-T1001 looks very sad as it stands within the premises of Arlington Motors in early May summer sunshine. There were three such vehicles built, being part of a larger programme of sixteen in total made up of both double and single deck examples, with the intention of replacing earlier types then in everyday use. In the event only nine were ever built. Design work had started in 1928 but many technical problems were encountered and it was not until the period 1930/31 that the finished vehicles appeared. In the meantime AEC was mass producing its Regal, Regent and Renown chassis which put paid to any further development of these LGOC built vehicles and large orders for all three of the AEC types were placed instead. The single deck vehicles were always associated with the routes from Kingston out to Weybridge and Woking. (K.A.V.Newley)

STL2662 is parked beside the High Wycombe garage building which still stands to this day albeit much altered. Front route blinds are set for a journey on Route 362B to Penn Post Office and running plates HE5 are carried. The bus is interesting being one of only four whose chassis were built in 1941 as 17STL sub-class and which carried STL11 bodies built in 1936 by the LPTB. The others were STL2655, 2656 and 2659. Certain modifications were necessary to the bodies for them to be married up to the crash gearbox fitted AEC Regent chassis and the resultant vehicles were classified 17STL11/1. (J.F.Higham)

LT61 photographed at Pimlico on a very dismal December day operates from Potters Bar garage on Route 134. This is a strange picture since the angle of the wheels suggest the bus is heading for the railings but the passengers seem more interested in the photographer than where they are going so perhaps all is well. The paper sticker beneath the running number plates gives details of the proposed Christmas services for the route. Normal service will operate on Tuesday 24th December while on Christmas Day there will be a service between Victoria and Potters Bar garage until about 4 o'clock after which there will be no service. On Boxing Day a Sunday service will operate. All very different from what can be expected at Christmases nowadays. (G.F.Ashwell)

The worst weather in south east England since 1939 occurred on the weekend of March 2nd and 3rd. Here a small Leyland C type has been halted by a snowdrift near Tatsfield on the Croydon to Westerham road and one of the service vehicles converted from a T class bus has come to the rescue. Although the particular Cub involved in the incident is unknown the route it had been operating on is clearly evident.

(The Illustrated London News Picture Library)

LT400 photographed at the Wake Arms, Epping Forest, to which point Route 38 was extended on Sundays starting on 26th May. This was the first time since 1942 that the route had made the journey beyond the Royal Forest Hotel at Chingford. In the background an Enfield T waits on Route 242. Leyton garage proved to be the last operational home for this LT, the bus being withdrawn and passed to R.L.Daniels for scrap in May 1949. (C.Carter)

The original identity of this former ST remains a mystery at present but it could be either ST337, 777 or 798, all of which were disposed of to the Royal Navy in 1942 or 1943. A clue as to which it is could be in its Navy identity number - RN17787. A considerable amount of work has been carried out on the exterior of the bus including the fitment of a neatly executed driver's cab door. The overhang to the front roof has been removed and some sort of ventilation intake added to the front dome. The tyres now look somewhat dejected but must have been a picture originally when some "bull happy" naval officer ordered the walls to be painted white. The background to the picture looks nautical and may be some sort of ship with ventilation shaft funnels protruding above a lifeboat. (L.Housden collection)

Leyton garaged LT51 is parked with another visible behind the low wall at the Green Man, Leytonstone, with blinds showing it to be working the northern section of Route 10 out to Abridge. The use of curviform panels and cut outs to the upper deck entrance was a very pleasing feature of these bodies. The route however was destined to receive the first post-war RTs in the following year. (W.J.Haynes)

Green Line route 723 commenced operation on 6th March and TF73c returned to passenger service in the same month operating from Grays garage. It had previously seen duty as an ambulance being converted for this role in September 1939 just two months after first entering service from Romford, London Road garage on the East London network of Green Line services. In this view taken at Minories coach station, Aldgate, the coach stands in front of T712c from Epping garage on route 720 which was introduced a month earlier than the 723. Of special note is the short lived white on black type of blind initially used on the re-introduced services. (J.F.Higham)

When compared to the view of T207 which appeared in the 1948 book some small differences can be detected with this view of the same bus taken some two years earlier. In this picture the bus carries the small "b" after its fleet number indicating its use within the Country Area. Also fitted are restricted lenses to the side lights and a shallower life guard. The stalk fitted to the top of the nearside front mudguard is still in place while the vehicle operates from Windsor garage on route 458 from its stand here at Uxbridge to Slough. At the very end of the year the bus was pressed into use in the Central Area as can be seen later in this book. (K.A.V.Newley)

Green and white liveried CR17b and just distinguishable CR16b await use as rush hour relief vehicles during the summer. Whilst some routes received comfortable 9T9 coaches for this purpose nine routes including the 133 received these diminutive and somewhat erratic rear engined Cubs. By the end of this year public transport mileage in London exceeded that of the immediate pre-war level with a fleet which included many obsolete and ill-maintained vehicles. Close examination of the roof area of CR17b demonstrates the latter point. Route 133 was normally operated by the STL class from Croydon and Streatham garages. (W.J.Haynes)

None of the LTs or STLs can be positively identified in this view but the street furniture, advertising and taxi cabs add to this very interesting general view. The Eros statue still has to be replaced but one of the advertising screens exhorts you to join the Palestine Police, "a man's job for £20 a month and all found"! You can visit the London Pavilion for a showing of the Gregory Peck blockbuster feature film six times a day starting at 10.15 a.m. and then, if your fancy takes you, you can purchase a piece of jewellery from Saqui and Lawrence, whose premises stand beneath the Schweppes advertising. (V.C.Jones/Ian Allan)

STL555, one of the ex-open top C.H.Pickup vehicles given ill matching top decks by London Transport waits on the Shoreditch stand of route 47 in May. Much detail of this vehicle's history appears with a photograph in the 1948 book of this series but this can be expanded with some further facts. The five STLs taken over from this operator were given LPTB classification 12STL8 or 1/12STL8. The differing chassis code was allocated due to different braking systems being fitted. Body numbers were allocated in sequence with fleet numbers and were 14281 to 14285 and except for STL553 which received a later STL12 body in April 1947 the others always operated married to their original chassis. Note the non-standard seat backs just inside the lower saloon. (G.F.Ashwell)

The ultimate Daimler to be fitted with the manufacturer's own six cylinder engine was D181 delivered to the LPTB and put into service in March 1946. In 1950 the engine would be exchanged for an AEC unit. Pictured in Great Castle Street, a stone's throw from Oxford Circus while working "swinger" duties on Route 88, the conductor has a friendly chat with her driver before they return south to Clapham Common. A pre-war Leyland Titan TD4 in the shape of STD45 is employed on Route 113 and departs in the opposite direction to Edgware. (Omnibus Society)

A busy bus scene in Liverpool Street with lead vehicle STL1118 from Dalston garage operating on Route 11 to Shepherds Bush alongside the blackened buildings beneath Broad Street Station. The conductor of the STL converses with the Inspector while another STL on Route 11 waits in the road to take up the space which will be left by the LT pulling out on route 9 to Mortlake. (R.F.Mack)

ST856 stands devoid of any exterior advertising or indication of its raison d'etre while resting beside summer greenery in an unidentified location. In the 1948 book of this series a picture appears of the bus in service on route 11 clothed in advertising but having lost its offside headlamp assembly which was by then replaced with a metal patch. (W.J.Haynes)

The first order for the AEC Regal chassis placed by the LGOC in 1929 called for fifty chassis which were given fleet numbers T1 to T50. All except T38 were bodied by the LGOC with 30 seat rear entrance bodies. The offside at least has not changed much in this view of T43 taken seventeen years later. The first three windows of the saloon were originally of the half drop opening type with glass louvres above. The deeper low rail moulding was probably added when the body received its first overhaul. In its present condition it is seen arriving at the obsolete Green Line coach stop used as an alighting point at Chingford, Royal Forest Hotel, while operating on Route 205 from Enfield garage. Note the black painted top to the radiator and the still masked lenses to the side lights. (W.J.Haynes)

RT38 is pictured on Route 74 displaying the short working terminal of Marylebone. Note the use of the nearside route number plate by the platform and the provision of a route stencil holder above the adjacent window. First entering service on 3rd January 1940 and now much in need of a complete overhaul, this was the bus which would be selected after its overhaul to become a trainer for the new post-war RTs. It was sent first to Leyton garage in February 1947 and later to Potters Bar garage ahead of those garages receiving their new vehicles.

Operating as P22 on Route 53A to Plumstead Common, ST375 represents a typical standard vehicle from this class. Of the 1140 vehicles which were classified ST at one time or another, well over 800 of the bodies were practically of the same design as shown here, being built by the LGOC, Strachans and Short Brothers. Note the chestnut paling fence which was probably provided in lieu of the metal railings removed from the front of the houses for the war effort. (J.G.S.Smith collection)

STL325 stands within the small outside parking area in the confines of St.Albans garage while taking a rest from its duties on Route 84 which has brought it from Arnos Grove and to where in due course it will return. This was one of the 6STL3 type which remained petrol engined throughout its life being fitted with a unit removed from the LT class when they were converted to oil. Potters Bar garage used this type on the long country run up the A6 and they had a very distinctive engine sound, often accompanied by a certain amount of backfiring. The 1936 built garage, now closed and much vandalized, still stands and a group of dedicated people are hard at work trying to save it as a centre for preservation and bus heritage. (W.J.Haynes)

Normally a double deck operation, Route 409 operating between West Croydon and Forest Row, plays host to Q75b which is seen at West Croydon prior to making a journey as far as East Grinstead. The picture illustrates the riding qualities and problems which would have been experienced on roadway surfaces of stone setts which were not uncommon in 1946.

When the Green Line routes from Aldgate to Brentwood and Hornchurch were reintroduced as 721 and 722 on 6th March and 3rd April respectively the TFs used before the war did not reappear. Instead new Daimler CWA6 double deck vehicles with 56 seat Duple bodies were allocated to the re-opened Romford, London Road garage. Whilst being to relaxed utility specification, their upholstered seats were not what could be termed coach standard and since most of the Bow and Whitechapel Roads were still granite setts at the time, the comfort of the ride offered hardly fitted the Green Line image. In its initial condition with green and white livery and white on black blinds, D159 waits at Aldgate.

This ex-NS bus is easily identifiable with its registration number XO4078, staff canteen service fleet number 32H and still carrying its original bonnet side plate embossed NS429. So far the location has defied identification. One small clue is that the building immediately behind has "Block D" on a metal plate affixed to the brickwork, a practice often carried out on the Peabody Trust Estates. Neither is it known if the canteen is passing through or simply parked in an awkward fashion on the corner of the road junction. (L.Housden collection)

Castle Coaches of Lewisham acquired ex-TF1 in February of the year under review and quickly made use of the Green Line brackets to add their own details. The coach had been disposed of by LPTB to Henry Lane, dealers of Chelsea, quickly passing to its new operator still wearing London Transport livery. The body, number 18075, was designed and built at Chiswick Works in 1937 and originally had a rather different cab utilizing more glass. This was rebuilt to something nearer to standard 2TF2 configuration in June 1940. The chassis was a much modified Leyland Tiger being given the identification FEC with the Leyland six-cylinder 8.6 litre engine again much modified and mounted on its side under the floor on the offside of the chassis assembly. A fluid flywheel coupled to an electro-pneumatic gearbox, operated like that of the RT class, connected to the single rear driving wheels. (G.F.Ashwell)

STL2615 was garaged at Luton for some years prior to it being withdrawn from service in November 1948, its chassis being required for conversion to SRT17 and this STL16 body, number 193, eventually finding its way on to the chassis of STL2153. The bus is seen carrying WA garage plates indicating it had probably finished scheduled work the previous evening away from its home base on the long haul 321 route. The scene is Uxbridge Station which judging by the pictures found for this volume was a favourite venue for the bus photographers of 1946. The inadequate wartime type of bus shelter is also much in evidence here. (Michael Rooum)

Passengers appear to be boarding LT1388 on Route 38 opposite the Royal Forest Hotel at Chingford which suggests it has worked through from the Wake Arms on the summer Sunday extension which was re-introduced for the first time after the war on 26th May. The side blind over the platform dates from before 5th May 1943 which was when the 38 was re-routed via Pembury Road instead of serving Hackney and Graham Road. For some time during the war years this bus operated in brown livery as did several others because of a shortage of red paint. Leyton garage would be the last home of this vehicle which was withdrawn from service in September 1947. (L.Housden collection)

Crystal Palace Parade is a bleak place at the best of times but here it is seen at its most uninviting as STL60 takes its layover while working Route 94. Both Bromley and Catford garages used STL class vehicles on this route and the leading bus, with blinds set for the journey to Southborough, is garaged at the former. (D.W.K.Jones)

D172 on Route 722 takes a well earned rest at the Minories bus and coach station, Aldgate, after negotiating the road setts common then to the East End of London. The vehicle though carrying Green Line badges is painted in Country Area colours of green and white with a brown roof. Of note is the full use of the route aperture, the Central Area Ds never being seen without the bottom quarter being blanked off. The Duple manufactured body, whilst to "austerity" specification is nicely proportioned. The trolleybus just visible on the left of the picture is prophetically displaying an incorrect 695 route blind over the platform, the last lines of which read "SEVEN KINGS, GOODMAYES". The 663 route on which the vehicle is working did not reach these points until 1959, some thirteen years later. (J.F.Higham)

T458c complete with painted radiator surround and fitted with the first post-war type of Green Line blind and white lettered side boards, stands outside Amersham garage. Within the garage the front of C15 can also be viewed which together dates the photograph as being taken in April, the month the Green Line route was introduced. In the 1952 book of this series the same T class vehicle can be seen after having received Central Area livery. (A.B.Cross)

Seen standing on the perimeter of the skid patch at Chiswick Works, STD127 is ready to be despatched to Victoria garage to enter service from there in October. The chromium plated radiator surrounds were a distinguishing feature of this batch of STDs which was perpetuated on the first batch of the single deck TD class. These handsome vehicles were purchased as a temporary measure, the promised RT class not appearing in bulk until the summer of 1947. (LT Museum 18378)

Although not having the clarity expected within this series of books, it was thought that this picture should be included from a historical and rarity point of view. Route 147 had its origins in a route 248 started on 30th August 1933 between Ilford and Leytonstone via Gants Hill. Renumbered 147 on 3rd October 1934 it was re-routed via The Drive on 3rd July 1935. During the war it was curtailed on two occasions at Wanstead Lane. The first on 20th November 1940 resuming through to Leytonstone on 29th October 1941 and then on 16th June 1942. This curtailment lasted right through until 5th May 1948 when an extension as far as Redbridge Station was introduced. LT675 of Seven Kings garage is pictured at the "Wanstead Lane" terminus and in 1946 this seven minute run used three buses on Monday to Friday and two on Saturday. (R.Burrell)

The Kings Cross Coach Station situated in Crestfield Street was used initially as the London terminus for Green Line Route 727 from Luton on its inception on 29th May. The route however soon moved to the temporary coach station in Judd Street. Luton garaged TF16c disgorges its passengers while an official tries to sort out some problem with some agitated looking travellers. It is not clear whether the dog belongs to them, the service personnel or is just a local stray. The coach had been reconverted for passenger service in March from its temporary use as an ambulance. The second type of post-war Green Line blind is carried which has white lettering on black in the layout very shortly to be used on the familiar black on yellow variety. (Omnibus Society)

An interesting view of STL2696 standing alongside the Post Office in Market Street, Watford with another of the batch at the bus stop on the other side of the road. A Michelin tyre advertisement is carried in the space between decks as there was no provision for rear destination blinds on these vehicles which entered service in January and February. The white disc was still added to newly delivered vehicles and was perpetuated into 1947 with RT deliveries. It always seemed odd that the white band above the windscreen was not carried around the off-side to meet the white of the lower saloon windows. This is a detail missed on the recent excellent Corgi model of these buses. (Omnibus Society)

Standing beside some wartime ARP shelters, LT11 from Loughton garage with LT68 parked close behind, awaits further use on Route 10A. Both these open staircased LTs had moved to other garages by the time they were withdrawn from service in March 1949, LT68 then gaining further use as a learner bus until November 1949. For many years the trunk route 10 was associated with north-east London stretching out at times as far as Ongar while the 10A covered the road through Buckhurst Hill to Loughton and Epping first appearing in 1913. (R.Burrell)

A varied selection of differently bodied STLs together with two STs, two "Bluebird" LTs and a solitary G class vehicle make up an interesting panoramic view. This is the yard in Minories backing on to Aldgate Bus and Coach Station in which the poles supporting the trolleybus wires can just be seen. These are off-peak layovers, a relic of wartime operations and routes 15, 23, 25B and 25C can be discerned. The second STL from the left is showing a 25C blind which was the extremely rarely photographed variant of 25B which ran from Victoria to North Woolwich at its fullest extent. This particular STL is STL2193 and the only other identifiable vehicle is second from the right which is STL1663. (L.Housden collection)

ST1139 was a common sight along the Windsor - Slough - Langley corridor while in use on Route 417. It operated from Windsor garage for around two years commencing soon after its return from exile to Coventry Corporation during the war years and before being withdrawn from service in September 1948. This bus had an interesting early history, being one of the first nine Regent chassis built by AEC and which were bodied by Short Bros. of Rochester with open staircase 51 seat bodies in 1929. The LGOC were actively engaged in developing a new style of body themselves for the Regent chassis and so UU6610, as a demonstration vehicle, was handed over to the subsidiary East Surrey Traction Co. at Reigate. Later it moved on to Autocar Ltd. of Tunbridge Wells returning to Chiswick in December 1929. It was then purchased by the LGOC and returned to Autocar before moving on to East Surrey again in June 1930 where it gained fleet number 255. East Surrey became part of London General Country Services Ltd. in 1932 and when LGCS was compulsorily acquired by LPTB on 1st July 1933 the bus became ST1139. Although carrying the lowest chassis number in the ST class it carried what was then the highest fleet number.

Bushes occupy the site of the present day Uxbridge garage as T452 waits before continuing its journey to West Drayton on Route 223. This Country Area bus now finds itself on loan to Uxbridge garage having been re-converted for passenger service in December 1945 from its previous wartime use as an ambulance. The class identification of these 1936 Weymann bodied oil engined AEC Regals was 9T9 and the batch of fifty identical vehicles were numbered T403 to T452 with registrations CLX551-575 and CXX151-175 respectively.

Red liveried C14 is pictured in peaceful surroundings as it makes its way to Oxted Station by way of Route 464 working from Chelsham garage. Although the batch C2b to C75b were built for the Country Area, one of them, C51, became a Central Area bus in 1935. Ten more were repainted red in 1942 including this one but all this later group were returned to their original livery in later years and C14's turn came as late as December 1951 only for it to be withdrawn from service two years later. (W.J.Haynes)

Petrol engined T301 which originally entered service as a coach in February 1931 operating from Tunbridge Wells garage on the Green Line service to Oxford Circus was used in this capacity until the whole batch, T207 - T306 were replaced by the much improved 10T10 class in 1938/9. Stored after withdrawal from service, it was not used again until September 1939 when it was converted for use as a staff ambulance, given the service fleet number 423W and repainted into Chiswick green. Made redundant with the cessation of hostilities in 1945 it was then reconverted for passenger use as a bus in November 1945 and eventually allocated to Luton garage. It is pictured here emerging from the gloomy interior of the garage using the side doorway with blinds which show a long lost route number in this area, 376. This operated from Luton, Park Square to Kensworth, a village close to Whipsnade Zoo. The route was merged with the 364 from Hitchin in 1959, the 376 section becoming 364A. (A.B.Cross)

The twenty-four vehicles of the LTC class were Weymann bodied private hire coaches and as delivered had seating for either 28 or 30 passengers. The reason for this discrepancy is not certain but the 28 seat examples were brought into line by the addition of two seats around February 1938. Registration numbers ran in sequence from EGO505 and all twenty-four vehicles retained their original bodies which were numbered 17610 to 17633. LTC16 shown here is one of the ten which were built without a sunshine roof and in this view it is parked with other coaches soon after their return from wartime duties as ambulances. (K.A.V.Newley collection)

In the early summer months at Grays ST167 shows off its new Country Area colours which it received in October 1945 having always previously been a red bus. New in April 1930 it was put to work together with a large number of others of the class from Hammersmith garage. Converted to operate with a producer-gas trailer from June 1943 until November 1944, it was eventually withdrawn from service in November 1948 and its body was scrapped in January 1949, the chassis meeting a similar fate in the following month. (A.B.Cross)

G139 was delivered to the LPTB in June 1945 in a colour scheme of brown and yellow with a pinkish-brown roof. Here, still carrying this colour scheme, a number of passengers have availed themselves of a journey on this Park Royal bodied Guy Arab II with moquette seating. Photographed at the Royal Forest Hotel, Chingford, before departure to Dagenham, New Road, on Route 145 one has to wonder how effective the modest headlights proved in use during the hours of darkness particularly bearing in mind that there were no street lights on the stretch of road up to the Royal Forest Hotel. (W.J.Haynes)

This splendid view of High Wycombe garage nestling at the foot of Daws Hill includes for good measure Q209 fitted with Green Line blinds for Route 724 and an STL of the unfrozen variety parked within the garage. The liberal use of white paint extends right across the picture while the non plastic keep left bollards are a reminder of a bygone age. How tranquil it is compared to the frenetic traffic experienced at this spot today. (W.J.Haynes)

STL834 originally entered service in August 1935 carrying an STL5/1 body and received two body changes for similar types before becoming a war damage casualty in 1944. At the same time "Tunnel" STL1854 received damage and for reasons which are uncertain the STL13 body was remounted on to the earlier chassis and then despatched to A.W.Watton of Biggleswade to be rebuilt. When it re-emerged in December 1944 it had lost its front opening upper deck windows and remained an oddity until withdrawn from service in June 1953. Here, in 1946, it waits at Bromley-by-Bow before working short to Poplar through the narrow streets which have now been swept away by the northern approach road to Blackwall Tunnel. (L.Housden collection)

LT1182 was operating from Sutton garage at the time of its withdrawal from service but prior to its transfer it was allocated to Tottenham garage and is seen here with duty plates AR4 as it works on Route 236 to Finsbury Park. The driver is obviously enjoying the attention being given to his bus and holds his summer headware in his hand to add a theatrical air to proceedings. (D.A.Ruddom collection)

ST951 looks in reasonable condition as it performs as a learner bus with a somewhat non-standard "L" plate. This was its sole use in its short lived post-war days. In December it was withdrawn from these duties to re-emerge in March 1947 in its new guise as 692J, a 7 ton mobile canteen. This was a service it performed for the following five and a half years and when eventually disposed of to Kirby Motors of London E14 in August 1952 it was over twenty one years old. (Lens of Sutton)

A nice study in rear ends (STL version) at Aldgate. STL342 with an LPTB built body dating from 1934 on the left shows the more curved profile compared to STL46 with a 1933 LGOC body of the squarer variety. The split rear platform window to STL342 is a wartime measure. The Acton Vale destination on Route 15 shows that the picture was taken either on a Sunday or a Bank Holiday. (L.Housden collection)

In 1946 the 74 was one of the few routes with an all-RT allocation which was provided by Putney Bridge garage. This made the ex-Tilling STs allocated to Holloway for the Marylebone Station to the Zoological Gardens additional service all the more incongruous. The crew of ST946 pose in old fashioned style with their bus while operating as J3 on this service. During the war years all the ex-Tilling STs which were serviceable were exiled to other parts of the British Isles for varying lengths of time and this ST spent July 1942 through to September 1944 on loan to Cheltenham and District Traction Company. Eventually withdrawn from service in July 1947 it was scrapped some two months later. (Lens of Sutton)

What must have been one of the earliest post-war cases of a double decker in use as a Green Line relief is depicted here by STL996b. Standing beside Victoria garage, the bus carries duty running plates WR94 and the neat sticker in the blind box indicates that earlier in the day it has made the journey from Windsor to central London via Slough. The body shown here was originally mounted on the chassis of STL974b but since September 1939 has graced this similar STL10, both buses having first entered service in 1935.

Battle weary T49, showing signs of a body split at the rear of the saloon doorway, stands at the Royal Forest Hotel, Chingford terminus of Route 205. The blind is set for the return journey to Hammond Street and passengers will board the bus guided by the white paint which still surrounds the entrance, a left-over from the days of the blackout. The bus had first entered service in January 1930 from Sutton garage to eventually end its days being dismantled by the LTE in April 1949. The blank space on the blind may be an indication of the fact that when the route was diverted in 1941 to Hammond Street instead of Potters Bar daily journeys worked from Loughton via Woodford Wells instead of the Royal Forest Hotel. These last operated on 21 May 1946 and so "Woodford Wells" may well be the obliterated via point. (A.B.Cross)

Before the war summer Sunday route 35A had operated to High Beach via Whipps Cross and Woodford Wells but when reinstated in 1946 it ran rather more as an extension of 35 beyond Chingford Hatch via Chingford, to which point it was eventually cut back from 1949 onwards. LT53 operating from Leyton garage pauses at Chingford Station as it makes its way to the terminus in the depths of Epping Forest carrying a good load of passengers aiming to enjoy the sylvan beauty and perhaps a pint in the Kings Oak. (A.B.Cross)

Leyton's "Bluebird" LT1290 arrives at the Royal Forest Hotel, Chingford, having completed its lengthy run from Victoria on Route 38. Later in the year the bus would be despatched to Mann Egerton of Norwich for renovation work on its visibly sagging body and on its return to service it would be garaged at Muswell Hill, not noted for many "Bluebird" allocations. (W.J.Haynes)

Duple bodied D140 entered service with the LPTB in January and it was built with the five opening window arrangement to each side and with a blind box above the platform. As with all the Central Area buses of the D class up to 181, it was garaged at Merton. The National Savings stamps advertised on the side of the bus were very popular at the time and the values of 6d (2½p), 2/6 (12½p) and 5/- (25p) show the very different value that money had in 1946. (S.L.Poole)

C61 began its service with London Transport at Addlestone garage in July 1935 and was last used in October 1953 from Chelsham. Afterwards it saw further service in Ceylon as a 41 seater, much increased from the 20 seat configuration it now operates as it picks up passengers in Westerham for the route 465 journey to Edenbridge. The fashions of the day look very smart despite the utility finish and the air of a sleepy country town is evident in this period piece. (Omnibus Society)

The unladen weight of STL84 is 6tons, 6cwts. as stated on the bodywork which makes it a lightweight when compared to modern day double deck buses. The vehicle is working on Route 133 from Croydon garage and is about to negotiate the Elephant & Castle junction. The "temporary" traffic signals worked by a policeman in a hut were a feature of this busy intersection for some years. Just to the left of the traffic signal a tramway pointsman operates his lever in a rather exposed position. (G.F.Ashwell)

Route 704 commenced operation on 6th March to work between Tunbridge Wells, where T553c is seen, through to Windsor. This Green Line liveried coach, a normal resident of WR garage, carries a TW garage plate having completed the previous evening's duties in this picturesque royal town. This photograph was taken in the Spring or early Summer, a fact confirmed by the first type of post war Green Line route blind carried by the coach which had re-entered passenger service in March. (Photobus)

STL218 entered service in September 1933 with an LGOC designed body of STL2 type numbered 13610. Over the passage of years the chassis received three further bodies from the same batch built at Chiswick and which entered service between August and December 1933 as STL203 to 252. On 7th October 1940, while operating from Forest Gate garage on Route 25B, the body was destroyed by enemy action. After the chassis had received attention at Chiswick it re-emerged with a float body of the STL12 type numbered 17908 and the resultant vehicle re-entered service in December 1940 lasting through to January 1950 when it was scrapped by Daniels of Rainham. Here it stands at the Leytonstone terminus of the Eastern Avenue route 66 while again working from Forest Gate garage. (R.Burrell)

Red liveried CR10 operating as AL1 in the first year of the resumption of racing at Epsom, which had been temporarily curtailed during the war years. The bus had previously been in store prior to being returned to service from Merton garage in the year under review. In April 1949 this CR received Country Area colours and can be seen in the 1951 book of this series. (Omnibus Society)

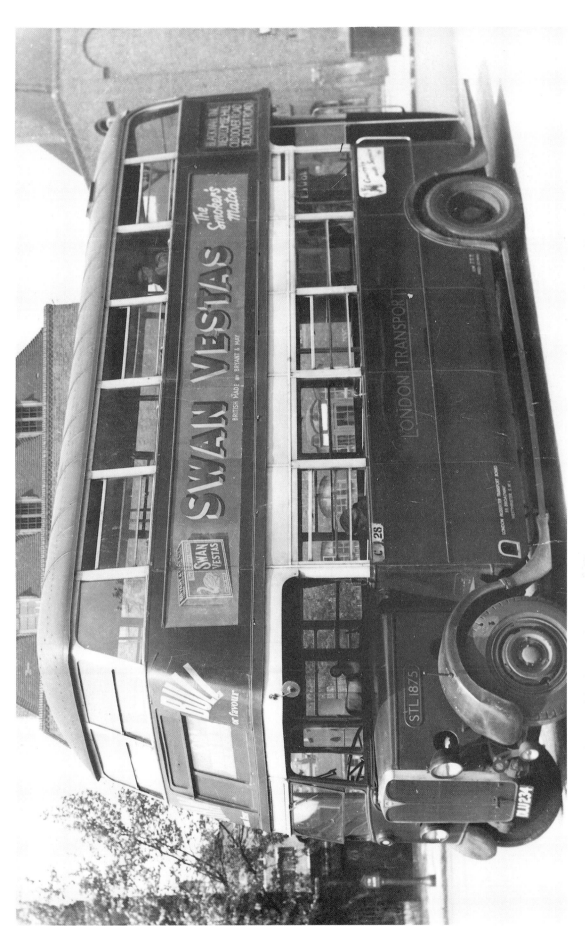

Forty of the STL class received special bodies with tapered upper decks designed to operate through the Blackwall and Rotherhithe Tunnels below the River Thames. They first entered service in March 1937 and most of their lives were spent working from Athol Street garage at Poplar. STL1875 waits at the Bromley-by-Bow terminus while working service 108A, which was a wartime introduction chiefly to serve the industry along Rochester Way at Eltham in the peak hours. On 13th February the service was introduced throughout the day on weekdays and a Sunday service appeared on 21st July in place of the "shorts" on 108 to Blackheath. The side blind is interesting, the last two lines of which read "Old Dover Road, Delacourt Road, Delacourt Road". This latter road was swept away by the A102(M) and nowadays Rochester Way would have to be reached via Kidbrooke Park Road. (J.Gascoine collection)

LT1205 still awaits attention to its boarded up windows in this view taken at the Royal Forest Hotel while STL2206 stands alongside. Both vehicles have arrived at this watering hole showing Chingford as the destination but the LT will eventually leave for Dagenham while the STL belonging to Enfield garage will head west on Route 102 to Golders Green. (J.Gascoine collection)

T255 in company with two early RTs and some STLs stands parked beside the railway line at Kingston on what is now the site of a new bus station. What is intriguing in this picture is the paint scheme on the front dome of RT108 parked immediately behind the single decker. The red has been carried down the upper deck corner pillars in the same fashion as on the post-war batch of STLs when they were delivered. Although the T carries route blinds for Hounslow route 81 the vehicle and the others are in fact out of use and stored. (R.Burrell)

Q114 waits at the Alexandra Park short working terminus before departing as WG2 on Route 233 to Finsbury Park. Neither the route stencil holder above the entrance or that fitted at the top of the first saloon window are being used on this Park Royal bodied 5Q5. First put into service from Dalston garage in March 1936 for use on Route 208, the bus found itself at West Green garage after the war eventually being replaced by a vehicle of the RF class in January 1953. In the background an LT and a Guy turn on the 144A/144B routes. (D.W.K.Jones)

Camberwell garaged STL1199 operates as Q12 on route 35 as it makes its way through the City en route to Clapham Common. The body is obviously of the basic STL5 variety but this is one of those rare occasions when the PSV Circle's excellent publications let you down! STL1199 lost the STL11 type body it had carried through the war in September 1945 but then the lines get crossed since another STL11 body, number 15596 is shown as being mounted and remaining until withdrawal in June 1950, whereas this is obviously an STL5 body. (K.A.V.Newley)

New to the London General Country Services in August 1932, JH4650 was one of twenty three petrol engined AEC Regents with LGOC 48 seat bodies of the design commonly known as "Bluebirds". These were a shortened version of that fitted to the last batch of the LT class. With the upper deck extended over the driver's cab a higher seating capacity could have been attained but this was restricted due to the weight restrictions then in force. The batch of vehicles were to be given registration numbers GX5314 to GX5336 and the first ten entered service carrying GX5314 to GX5323. However, the remaining vehicles were put into store and their registrations cancelled. During 1933 these vehicles entered service in two batches and received Surrey marks APC162 to APC170 and Hertfordshire marks JH4646 to JH4650 accordingly. During 1935 fleet number ST1084 was allocated to this vehicle and here in 1946 the bus is seen operating from Watford High Street garage in The Parade on Route 334A to Croxley Green (Manor Way). (J.G.S.Smith collection)

An early summer view depicts ST850 as it works the supplemental service to the Zoological Gardens on route 74. Holloway garage, who worked this schedule in 1946, seem to have received an allocation of ST7 type ex-Tilling open staircase buses specifically for this which is in line with the type of work usually given to these worn out vehicles. (S.A.Newman)

This photograph of ST141 clearly shows the rear end treatment of a Short Brothers lowbridge body of 1930 after much alteration by visits to Chiswick Works. Originally operated by the National Omnibus and Transport Company on the route between Watford and Chesham which was worked jointly with the Amersham and District Motor Haulage Co.Ltd., the bus is seen in 1946 still plying the same well worn track under the 336 number. It reached the end of its operating life in London when it was withdrawn from service in October 1952 and disposed of to a dealer by the name of Green who had premises in the Tooting area. This same vehicle appears in other views elsewhere in this book and a complete external survey is afforded to those who may have modelling interests. (Surfleet Transport Photographs)

The repositioned staircase and one of the two lower saloon emergency exits, in the form of a door built into the extreme rear of the offside, are easily discernible in this view of RT97 as fitted for "Pay As You Board" operation. The traditional colour scheme in which these vehicles were delivered is retained although the white area is carried to the rear of the lower deck windows to pleasing effect.

At the end of the year some Country Area 7T7s joined the band of single deckers providing relief on busy Central Area routes. T207b is seen at Crystal Palace still wearing its green livery and operating from Norwood garage. Earlier in the book the bus can be seen working in the Country Area from Windsor garage but following this snowy introduction it would remain in the Central Area for the last three and a half years of its life. (D.W.K.Jones)

Petrol engined T365 to T367 of 1932 build, which first carried Strachan or Harrington coach bodies, were rebodied in December 1938 with the Weymann bus bodies originally used to rebody AEC Reliances R44, R3 and R8 respectively. At the same time they were re-engined to diesel power but they never entered service in this form as later in the month the bodies and engines were transferred to T223, T237 and T234 to complete the thirty conversions of the 11T11 designated type. T223, which in its original form carried a Duple coach 30 seat body, entered service with the East Surrey Traction Company in January 1931. Here it is seen at Greenford in its final guise operating a short working on Route 211 which at its fullest extent ran between Ealing and Ruislip Lido. T365 to T367 were put back into their original condition before being disposed of early in 1939. (D.W.K.Jones)

ST1070 is pictured in Watford outside the main Post Office in Market Street awaiting a fresh crew from the High Street garage while working a short journey on route 321 to the Three Horseshoes at Garston, the main service to Luton being more usually the province of STLs. Originally operated by the LGCS and delivered new in August 1932 this vehicle was one of the two small batches numbered ST1032 to 1039 and ST1070 to 1084 which were built with LGOC bodies extending over the driver's cab and known as "Bluebird" STs. The lamp post just to the left of the picture still has a metal plate bearing a large S for shelter fixed to it which is a relic of the wartime years. (G.F.Ashwell)

T632, alias X201027 and named "Arkansas" while on temporary loan to the American Red Cross as a Clubmobile, is now back with its rightful owners at Chiswick Works in the early Spring. It awaits an overhaul and transformation back to something approaching its original condition when it first entered service in August 1938.

This picture poses a little bit of a puzzle. T491c was one of a number which had to receive attention by Northern Coachbuilders Ltd. of Newcastle upon Tyne after having sustained severe damage at Elmers End garage in the bomb incident on 18th July 1944. Records show that the vehicle was eventually returned and moved to Dunton Green on the 1st May 1946 being relicensed for duties on 15th May. However, this photograph is obviously posed at Chiswick Works and would seem to be taken to show the new style of two tone green Green Line livery, black on yellow blinds and gold leaf route boards which were introduced from June 1946 onwards. So the question is, in what state did it operate in May at Dunton Green?

ST1057 waits on the Enfield Town stand of Route 310 in Cecil Road with the Florida Cinema visible on the right and the trolleybus wires overhead leading into the terminal loop for the 629 via Sydney Road and back to London Road. This ST with a body by Short Bros. was one of a number originally operated by the East Surrey Traction Company of Reigate on behalf of the LGOC which accounts for its London registration. (J.G.S.Smith collection)

ST1101b operating as WA69 on the cross-Watford route 346 to Oxhey Hall Farm pulls away from a request stop in St.Albans Road. The front nearside dome shows signs of contact with Country Area trees. Originally numbered 229 in the East Surrey Traction Company's fleet the bus was numbered in the ST series upon acquisition by LPTB and classified 2/1ST9. The body code ST9 was given to all the various bodies on STs acquired from East Surrey and National and no particular identification was given to examples such as this which carried the distinctive square cab and different rear blind arrangement which marked it as a Ransomes, Sims and Jefferies product. (A.B.Cross)

NCME bodied G305 operates from Barking garage as it heads east on Route 23 to Becontree Heath. This Guy Arab only completed a little over five years service with London Transport before being withdrawn and sold to Edinburgh Corporation to receive a new eight feet wide Duple Midland (Nudd) body. It was then given a new chassis number, re-registered JWS586 and went on to spend the period to 1967 working in its new capital city north of the border. (S.A.Newman)

At present the identity of this ex-T remains a mystery but it is photographed with a backdrop of war damage in France. The route blind aperture has been fitted with a neat display which reads "ECOURT ARLEUX BUGNICOURT DOUAI". Douai is the town in north-east France in which the photograph of T263 in the 1948 book of this series was taken. (L.Housden collection)

The 18STL20 vehicles became a familiar sight in Watford following their delivery in January and February 1946 and STL2700 makes its way through the town on 9th July. Three of the buses (STL2683/4/5) were delivered in red livery to the same layout but received their true Country Area colours in October. None of the batch ever worked in the Central Area. (A.B.Cross)

In the last months of the war the lift bridge carrying Manor Way over King George V Dock entrance was severely damaged by a V2 rocket and thereafter Route 101 had to make a 1½ mile detour using private roads within the docks. In July 1946 two G type buses from Upton Park garage hurry along the concrete roadway past the Dry Dock at the western end of King George V Dock. It was to be another year before the bridge would be reopened and five buses saved from the 101 schedule. If you had tried to describe the 1996 view of Docklands to the workers dotted about this view you would probably have been regarded as barmy or at best a science fiction writer. (Docklands Museum)

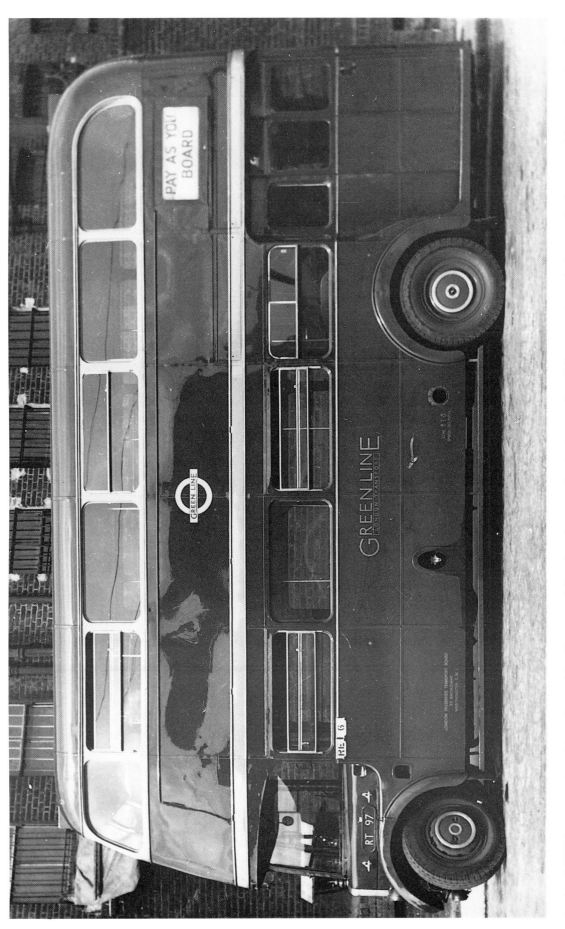

In April RT97 was repainted into Green Line livery and fitted with new wheel trims and a sliding opening window to the last nearside lower saloon bay in order to provide more ventilation for the conductor who sat behind it. Before the month was out the coach, which was the first RT to be finished in Green Line colours, entered service from Romford garage and it is seen at Aldgate working on Route 721. It shared the duties with vehicles of the D class which, although newer, gave a much inferior ride. The experiment as a "Pay As You Board" coach proved unpopular with passengers and this fact coupled with the unreliability of the ticket machinery, lead to the ordinary roving conductor being introduced in early July. The vehicle continued to operate in this condition until early 1947 when it moved into Chiswick Works to emerge two years later as RTC1. (A.B.Cross)

Complete with a full set of offside saloon window louvres, T391 is the sister vehicle to T392 shown elsewhere in this book in totally different surroundings. This bus managed to complete a further four years service with London Transport before being disposed of for scrap. The tape, which has been added to the roof, was a common sight on vehicles which let in the rain. The body built by Dodson, although of similar style to those of its contemporaries, was somewhat higher and the two vehicles were always easily recognisable because of this. Route 218 can be traced back to 4th January 1922 when a service 62 was introduced between Kingston and Shepperton using K type single deck buses. (J.G.S.Smith collection)

Providing a little relief to Route 96, C88 waits at the Red House, Wanstead terminus before running in to Forest Gate L.T.Garage at the end of the peak hour. A Putney Bridge RT behind rests before working the full route to Putney Common. C88 entered service from Enfield garage in May 1936, ending its revenue earning days at Chelsham still in Central Area livery in March 1951. (R.Burrell)

G6 is seen soon after having been repainted into standard LPTB Central Area livery of red and broken white from its previous colours of indian red and primrose. Officially Hanwell's Guys were allocated to Routes 83 and 83A while the 97 was the responsibility of the Bristols helped by a few LTs. However, as here, they often strayed on to the Greenford to Brentford route. This vehicle is turning short at the Ealing, Perivale Lane terminus. Only two opening windows are provided each side of the bus while the rear upper deck emergency window has a metal panel in place of the customary glass. (J.F.Higham)

LT53 splashes its way through flood water in the Lea Bridge Road while making its way to Victoria on Route 38A. Floods on this part of the road are not uncommon, probably due to the low lying nature of the land across the Lea Valley. Two trolleybuses on Routes 557 and 581 follow at a respectable distance. Presumably the photographer had his "wellies" on? (Greater London Record Office)

T512 returned to Green Line work in February having spent the period from September 1939 through to August 1945 in use as an ambulance. It was built in January 1938 and its first post-war outings were made from Epping garage on route 720 between Bishops Stortford and Aldgate, where this picture was taken. The route became the province of TF coaches in later years. (R.Burrell)

A favourite spot for bus photographers, the substantial mock-Tudor public house by the Iron Bridge at Hanwell, which at the moment rejoices in the name of 'McGinty's Irish Pub', forms the background to B22 on Route 92. The driver has already reset the blind for the return journey to Wembley. The batch of twenty buses numbered B10 to B29 delivered to the LPTB between October and December 1945 carried relaxed utility design Duple bodies on which the lower bonnet and PV2 radiator gave a much sleeker appearance than their 1942 predecessors. Powered by an AEC 7.7litre engine they gave good service to London Transport and several other operators for a lengthy period. (J.F.Higham)

Green liveried ST9 operates from Grays garage on the local Route 371A between Purfleet and Grays. Only ten such bodies for this class were ever built with blind box set into the driver's cab roof and all were withdrawn from service wearing Central Area red livery except for this example, which, carrying body number 12350, had received Country Area colours in December 1945 producing this unique combination. Its allocation to Grays was a result of its conversion to producer gas operation for a while during the war. (R.Burrell)

Brand new D186 is pictured on the forecourt of Morden Underground Station with an STL to keep it company on 12th May. The one hundred vehicles of the batch numbered from D182 had been purchased to help relieve the desperate need for new vehicles immediately after the war. In all essentials the chassis and mechanical parts were similar to the first of the class delivered in 1944 except for an improved radiator design. Bodies built by Park Royal were to a relaxed utility specification as demonstrated by the six opening windows and provision for full route blinds front and rear although the latter asset was never used. The first post-war livery in which these buses were delivered is clearly seen in this view. (J.H.Price collection)

Standing at Bromley North, STL117 appears to have its route blind set for a return journey on Route 146A to Keston but, as can be seen, there was not much room for error when rewinding the blind on these vehicles. In the opening month of the following year the bus would be transferred to Watford High Street garage in the Country Area, eventually to be repainted green and never again to be associated with its ancestral home. (W.J.Haynes)

The date is 30th March and Q234c is pictured in Allsop Place, Baker Street, before returning to its home town of Crawley on Route 710. A total of six of the 6Q6s were garaged at CY for use on this route, which was introduced on 6th March operating between Crawley and London via Horley, Salfords, Redhill, Hooley, Coulsdon, Croydon and Streatham as shown in white paint along the route board. All these Qs were replaced in the early summer months by 10T10 type coaches and they then joined thier counterparts at garages more associated with these vehicles. Their revolutionary design incorporated an engine mounted slightly inclined on the offside of the chassis driving through a fluid flywheel and four speed pre-selective gearbox to the offset rear axle. (A.B.Cross)

With Marble Arch just discernible in the background, STL1262 speeds past as it operates on route 16 from Cricklewood garage on 22nd April. The bus appears to have an identity problem, carrying the ST2 type body, number 12251 which was originally fitted to ST645 when that vehicle was new and on which some surgery has been performed by the transplant of a standard STL cab. Several pictures of this unique vehicle have been shown in earlier books of this series which allow the reader the opportunity to follow its history since the war years. The advertisements of the time have a unique flavour - who would have thought it patriotic to buy a bottle of Jeyes' Fluid! (L.Housden collection)

Seen outside the Law Courts on its journey to Liverpool Street on Route 11, ST75 operates with running plates D32. New in April 1930 the bus was eventually to be withdrawn from service in March 1949, having spent the period August 1943 through to November 1944 in use with a producer gas trailer. (R.Burrell)

ST530 was always recognisable in post-war years with its home made looking top deck which it gained after a "lowbridge incident" while on loan to Northern Roadways of Glasgow during the war. It also still has two blocked up windows as it operates from Dalston garage before its many transfers between garages until being withdrawn from passenger service in June 1948. A spell as a training vehicle from Cricklewood and later Camberwell garages followed before, in March 1949, the body number 10554 was scrapped followed by the chassis in June. (L.Housden collection)

Route 469 has pottered south westwards from Staines for many years, although this is the first view to appear in this series of books. Red ST704 waits at the Staines terminus before working as far as the Red Lion at Thorpe. The PSV Circle publication LT7 quotes this bus as receiving Country Area livery in August 1948 only to be returned to Central Area livery again in November 1948. Was it worth it you may well ask since in April 1949 it was withdrawn from service to be immediately despatched to the scrapyard of R.Daniels at Rainham. (W.J.Haynes)

Petrol engined STL57 makes its way across London Bridge for its home garage of Bromley via route 47 with some very interesting vehicles keeping it company. Although many body changes took place at overhaul time within the batch numbered STL51 through to STL130 and classified 8STL4, only two members, 59 and 75, managed to acquire bodies outside the Tilling variety shown in this photograph. Always LGOC owned but built and operated by Thomas Tilling Ltd. until the handover to LPTB on 1st October 1933, many of these buses lasted into LTE ownership. (J.G.S.Smith collection)

The open staircase "Tilling" variety of the ST class were well scattered among the operating garages of the LPTB at this period after complaints from the Union that conductresses did not like to be employed on a permanent basis on the type. The girls of Leyton, Loughton and Potters Bar presumably put up with the LTs! ST1025 is pictured operating from Holloway garage on the supplemental summer schedule of route 74 between Marylebone Station and the Zoological Gardens. After the summer operation of this additional service finished on 9th October the bus found itself in store before reappearing the following year operating from the familiar "Tilling" surroundings of Croydon garage. (W.J.Haynes)

Brand new D235 at Croydon Airport entered service in July from Sutton garage. The batch of one hundred vehicles coded 3/1D4 were purchased to help relieve the heavy demand for new vehicles immediately after the war. Delivered with six opening windows on each side set in pans, standard London Transport blind boxes and seating of moquette on tubular steel frames, the bodies were referred to as being to a "relaxed utility" specification. The evangelistic crusade advertised on the side of the bus seemed to draw its inspiration from the experiences of the recent war. (Lens of Sutton)

Green Line route 714 was introduced on 1st May 1946 to operate between London, Baker Street and Dorking via Hammersmith, Richmond, Kingston, Chessington, Leatherhead, Mickleham and Boxhill as indicated on the route board carried along the length of TF85c. The pre-war section of Green Line beyond Dorking to Horsham was not replaced. This photograph was taken after 29th May which was when the black on amber (or old gold or yellow if you prefer) destination blinds were introduced and gold lettering appeared on the route boards. (W.J.Haynes)

ST1 operates from Alperton garage in this view taken at Wembley High Road while it is engaged on Route 83 from Golders Green to Ealing. First of its class, delivered in 1929 hence the UU registration, it carries a later body than that with which it originally entered service. The white paper discs on the windows appear in several photographs of this period - can anyone remember what they were for? (J.G.S.Smith collection)

STL187 is seen operating as TC19 on route 133 on 24th July waiting to depart for South Croydon. The bus is standing in Liverpool Street and will leave via Old Broad Street. It was not until a year later that the 133 stand was moved to East Street with buses departing via Finsbury Circus and Moorgate. Originally this 2STL1 had entered service in July 1933 from Elmers End garage only to finish its operating career with London Transport in October 1947 garaged at Croydon, not many miles from its first home. (G.F.Ashwell)

STL2687 now carries advertising between decks as it works duty WA5 on Route 321 at Maple Cross. The conductor standing on the open platform wears a ticket punch which close examination shows to be the Effra Road variety used by London Transport Country Buses. This post-war batch of STLs classed 18STL20 were numbered from STL2682 through to STL2701 and carried registration numbers HGC215 - 234 and bodies 1059 to 1078 which always stayed together with the chassis on which they were mounted when manufactured by Weymann. (G.F.Ashwell)

Nearest the camera ex-T355 keeps company with well photographed T392 at the 125 Transit Camp situated at Hanover on 29th May. Both vehicles look in a neglected condition and interestingly T355 appears to have had some of its seating rearranged as the seat backs to two pairs can be seen through the windows immediately above the rear wheels, standing high and facing inwards. (J.H.Price)

ST1020 is seen at Windsor Castle on the local route 445 which ran from the town to Datchet Common. This ex-Tilling open staircase bodied vehicle carried the body code ST7 which was given to all the 52 seat vehicles which were numbered in the ST series from this, the largest independent operator taken over at the formation of the LPTB. This bus had been on loan to Central SMT of Motherwell, moving on to Northern Roadways of Glasgow between 1942 and 1944. In 1946 it is recorded as being a staff bus at Chelverton Road and a trainer at Hounslow, so it would appear to be a very temporary loan to cover a vehicle shortage at Windsor garage. (J.F.Higham)

This is the second picture in this book of former T392 and is taken at the Hanover Garrison HQ at the Robert Koch Platz. Compared to the earlier picture no military number is now carried but the bus looks as though a lick of paint has been applied. (J.H.Price)

CR28 operating on Route 73 to Kings Cross follows an LT class vehicle working through to Stoke Newington on the same route along Margaret Street, which at this point intersects with Regent Street. Obviously a diversion to avoid Oxford Circus is in operation. The rear view of the car shows admirably the pull down type of boot compartment lid and small sized rear windows then in favour. (Omnibus Society)

In June 1938 T543c entered service from East Grinstead garage being used on Green Line services H1 and H2 which operated from the town to Luton or Dunstable respectively. During September 1939 the coach was converted to an ambulance and in this capacity saw out the war years until in August 1945 it was reconverted for use in its intended role. Godstone garage is now the home of the coach and it is seen in the vicinity of Baker Street while in use on Route 709, an hourly service to Caterham Station which commenced on 6th March using 6Q6 coaches. This view is later in the year by which time 10T10 coaches had taken over the service and the familiar black on yellow blinds had appeared. The body, built by LPTB of composite metal and wood construction, is of the T10 type with glazed partition behind the entrance and wider doorway. (L.Housden collection)

As mentioned elsewhere, bus photographers in 1946 seemed a little limited in their choice of location. This is the Royal Forest Hotel at Chingford yet again, this time with Park Royal bodied G338 clearly demonstrating the glass emergency window fitted to the rear of the upper deck. This batch of vehicles from the West London body manufacturer consisted of G319 through to G357 although two sub-class identifications were involved, this particular vehicle being of the 1/3G8/2 variety. The bus, operated by Upton Park garage who had a small weekday allocation on this route, waits to continue its duties as U5 on the 145 to Dagenham, New Road. (A.B.Cross)

Standing within the Minories coach station, with an early style of sideboard for Green Line route 723, TF79 looks very smart after its recent refurbishment although at this stage the livery is green and white rather than the later two-tone green. The route blind appears to be blank and no duty number is carried which suggests this might be just prior to the 723 route's reintroduction on 6th March and some form of route familiarisation is being carried out. The production batch of TF Green Line coaches carried LPTB bodies built at their Chiswick Works and all were completed in 1939. They differed from the private hire version in that they had fixed roofs and no cant-rail windows.

Converted to an ambulance in September 1939, T515c was then reconverted for passenger use in November. Further need for public ambulances arose in 1940 and in May the coach again found itself in this alien role. In this view the vehicle, with its Emergency Medical Services insignia, shows the considerable damage sustained sometime near the end of hostilities, the roof and nearside having been ripped open allowing adverse weather to further add to its misery. After substantial rebuilding the coach was again in use and returned to passenger service in September 1945.

Q type buses first appeared on Route 230 in 1936 replacing much older S class vehicles and were the mainstay of the route until October 1942 when it was partially converted to double deck operation using lowbridge STL class vehicles. The route was always the responsibility of Harrow Weald garage from where Q160 is operating in this photograph. Full wartime blackout and passenger safety precautions are carried on this Park Royal bodied vehicle which had operated from the same garage since entering service in June 1936. (Omnibus Society)

STD103 is seen travelling west in Knightsbridge on Monday 24th August 1942, only having been placed into service the previous May. The bus, one of eleven similar vehicles operated by Victoria garage, is seen on Route 22 which plied between Homerton and Putney Common for seventy four years until finally losing its north London section in 1990. It is an unusual working for this type in 1942, as they were officially allocated to route 10 until 25th October 1944 when the type took over the Monday to Saturday duties on the 22. The angular wood framed body built by Park Royal is mounted on an "unfrozen" Leyland TD7 chassis having been manufactured from existing spare parts and the minimum of newly produced components which had been authorised and allocated by the Ministry of War Transport. (F.Willis)

Before the Second World War Green Line routes were identified by an alphabetical sequence, going through three different schemes during the thirties. When the Government decided on a resumption of Green Line services to alleviate bomb damage interruptions on the railways, a simple numerical system of route numbering was introduced. This started on 4th December 1940. All routes terminated in Central London and numbers went from 2 to 59 clockwise from Gravesend round to Grays. Care was taken not to duplicate Central Area route numbers over any road. Route 23 operated between Ascot and Victoria. STL1274 with STL11 type body number 15622 is seen here loading up for its journey to the home of the famous racecourse. It had been one of a number of Central Area buses of this class standing idle due to service cuts and was repainted and given its new role in June 1941. Since all these services were withdrawn on 29th September 1942 the date of this photograph can be narrowed down very nicely.

Eventually to be withdrawn from service in November 1948, LT636, a 1/2LT3/3, operates the first duty out of Nunhead garage on Route 63. The provision of anti blast netting is spasmodic but the masked headlights are still in place. The sticker below the running number plates advertises a flag day for sailors. (W.J.Haynes)

T651, photographed at Sevenoaks bus station, displays the unusual "To & From" inscription on the double ended blind which was occasionally favoured by the Country Area. Although working Route 404 which ran between Sevenoaks and Shoreham Village lying around four miles to the north, just off the A225, the bus is parked at the 413/454 boarding point. A lady, well protected from the elements and armed with a gamp converses with the male and female crew.

After an initial period from October 1944 in Pay As You Board use on Route 65, STL1793, the first of the experimental vehicles involved in this type of fare collection, languished out of service for two months before being reallocated to Dalston garage in May 1945. This picture taken at Liverpool Street proves its use in service on Route 11 with running plates D2, although it is thought to have probably employed a normal mobile conductor at this time. The clever use of the area above the offside rear wheel arch to build the staircase and the placing of inward facing bench seating in the rear portion of the lower deck allowed the normal seating capacity of 56 to be maintained. In August 1945 the bus was again transferred, this time to the Country Area at Reigate garage before the body, number 17722, was removed and scrapped in September 1947 being replaced by a standard STL14 type.
(L.Housden collection)

The date is 22nd June 1942 and bomb blasted STD92 with a further member of the class is pictured in Princes Street on the Oxford Circus stand awaiting return to the suburbs. The bus had entered service in June 1937 being one of a small batch of ten vehicles comprising a Leyland TD4c chassis fitted with standard Lysholm-Smith torque converter transmission, commonly referred to as a gearless bus, with only a brake and accelerator pedal. They were classified 2STD1/1. The body, which was also built by Leyland, seated 55 passengers. Due to excessive fuel consumption they were converted to standard TD4 configuration upon their first overhaul at which time they were also reseated to the more normal standard 56 and finished their days as 1STD1/1s. This particular bus spent its entire passenger carrying career at Hendon garage, only moving to pastures new as a learner vehicle in 1954. (F.Willis)

STL881 waiting during the war years on the Oxford Road stand above the railway at Putney for its scheduled time to return to Hornsey Rise. The background to this 1/9STL5 remained unchanged for many years and appears in some of the later years in this series of books. This chassis and body, number 15255, came together in January 1939 and were to stay married until eventually the bus was withdrawn from passenger service in December 1949. The driver's cab appears to have recently received a nasty dent. The Windsmoor coats advertisement is interesting since it apparently ignores the problem of clothes rationing which had been introduced in the Spring of 1942. It was reckoned that seven year's worth of coupons were needed for a new topcoat.

An interesting comparison in bodywork styles is provided by these two Qs at the stop opposite St.Albans garage. Q92, the lead vehicle, is a product of the Birmingham Railway Carriage & Wagon Company. It was originally built as a country area bus, later converted and used on Green Line work but is now back in use as first intended in green and white livery. Q236, the further of the two, is bodied by Park Royal for use as a Green Line coach and is finished in the two shades of green it was given upon its return to passenger service from long term use as an ambulance during World War II. Here it is in use on bus work on Route 355 from Harpenden to Radlett while Q92 is engaged on Route 365 which operated between Luton, St.Albans and Hill End. (Vanguard Bus Prints)

It appears that the Daily Graphic are sponsoring a visit to the Bertram Mills Circus at Olympia for the children of Wandsworth. ST687 is being used as a mobile advertising hoarding for this good deed and is about to pick the children up at Wandsworth Town Hall. It is as well the driver did not back his vehicle any further however. It would appear from the warm clothing that the Circus might be a Christmas treat for at least the 48 youngsters the bus will seat.

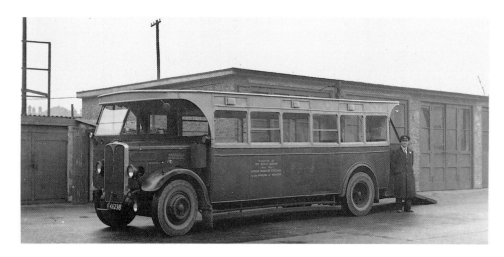

A single deck Tilling ST must have been unique although it must be admitted that it was never in service as such and it was only after the bus had been withdrawn from service in May 1948 that the conversion took place. The inscription on the side panel of ST962 reads "Presented by the British Legion and the London Transport Executive to the Ministry of Pensions". One can only presume LTE undertook the rebuilding and any further information on this vehicle in its new guise would be much appreciated. (A.D.Packer)

Surrounded by a desert of bomb sites, ST373 stands in Bowles Road with Old Kent Road garage in the background, displaying the usual terminal for buses working into the garage. Other vehicles in view include a coach on loan to LTE for peak hour duties carrying the unmistakable LT insignia above the offside mudguard. (F.W.Ivey)

LT349 was severly damaged during the War and its body was rebuilt by Cardiff Corporation. This resulted in a unique appearance, the bus having squared off windows fitted with winding mechanism. Further renovation in 1946 was carried out by Mann Egerton of Norwich. Here it is parked in Nunhead garage between two more standard stable mates. Basically the body, number 12678, is of the LT5 style although now classified LT5/8. The bus spent its last revenue earning days at Old Kent Road garage before being used as a learner vehicle at Middle Row and eventually being despatched to R.L.Daniels in March 1950 for scrap. (R.Burrell)

A short period of two months was spent at Victoria garage by ST988 in 1948 and it is seen operating on Route 77A to Kings Cross as duty GM33. Just why and where the driver has abandoned his passengers is uncertain. By January of the following year the bus was withdrawn from service having visited a further two garages in the meantime.

ST1 receives a helpful tow from a 6½ ton towing vehicle carrying trade plate 975GC which makes it impossible to accurately identify its original ancestry. In addition the miniscule fleet number is not clear on this print. It is known that underneath the lorry body now fitted lies a T class chassis, many of which were used to make service vehicles in the 1939/40 period. (R.Wellings collection)

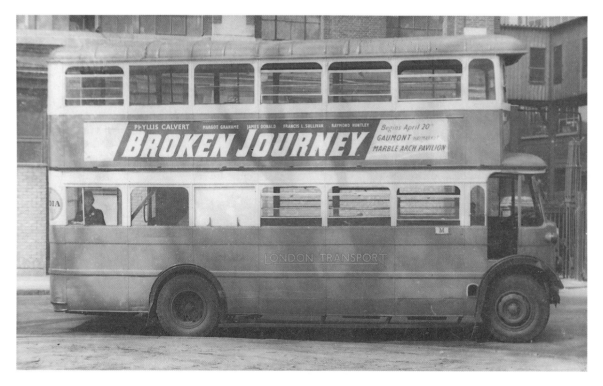

Only a few months before receiving attention by Berkeley Caravans of Biggleswade, ST404, parked at Brook Green, Hammersmith, appears in need of this attention to keep it going in service until January 1950. The Gaumont at the Haymarket and Marble Arch Pavilion will be showing the latest Phyllis Calvert film entitled Broken Journey beginning 20th April. The conductress keeps a wary eye on the photographer from a position where she may be required to make a few hand signals once the ST gets rolling. (David Jones collection)

The driver charged with delivering RT682 to London Transport left Park Royal Vehicles' works via Twyford Abbey Road instead of Abbey Road and the Piccadilly Line railway bridge neatly removed the roof. Here the vehicle stands back at the coachworks not only minus the roof but, not surprisingly, minus its driver. The result was that the bus entered service in July from Holloway garage several weeks after its contemporaries had been put to work from either Catford or Willesden garages. (LT Museum 18578)

Passing the Odeon Cinema which once stood at Shannon's Corner at the crossroads of the A3 and the B282, G169 is making its way to Esher operating from Alperton garage on their Sunday allocation on Route 72 when the route ran beyond its weekday terminus at East Acton to North Wembley. This picture raises a query with the records of the PSV Circle which state that the bus was repainted to red and broken white in August 1949. Here the bus has obviously received its repaint but the Sunday involvement of Alperton on the route ceased in April 1949! However, the wooden seats in the bus were replaced by upholstered units in August 1948 so perhaps that was when the brown livery was actually lost. (A.M.Wright)

This low angled view of T231 within its last six months of service clearly shows the poor condition of the exterior bodywork. Originally a Green Line 30 seat coach it was demoted to bus work in November 1938 with little alteration except for the replacement of the front destination box and the removal of the route board brackets. Pictured at Staines while operating on Route 218 from Kingston, it still wears its Country Area livery although it had seen service from a variety of Central Area garages. (David Jones collection)

Some of the buses used on Olympic Games special services are seen here at the Wembley sports complex on 31st July 1948. From left to right are Q167, RT274, T16, LTC4 with a further RT beside the LTC to complete the picture. Interestingly T16 carries a Putney Bridge garage plate. Prior to these special duties the bus had been garaged at Sidcup and afterwards was transferred to Kingston. (V.C.Jones)

Photographer Geoffrey Ashwell obviously seized the moment one day in April 1948 to take this neatly framed shot of Inter Station deck and a half Cub C106 helping out on Route 53A. In front is an LT and behind a former Western SMT Leyland Cheetah, CS3356, belonging to Ansell's Coaches both of which are working Route 12. Where, however, did Mr.Ashwell capture this evocative scene? Our theory is that this is St.George's Street, south of Hanover Square and the buses are on diversion. The pillar on the pavement is part of the portico of St.George's Church. (G.F.Ashwell)

A fine array of coaches provide a backcloth to LT1410 at Wembley Stadium while it is engaged on Olympic Games Official Transport duties. This was one of the last tasks performed by this sixteen year old vehicle which was withdrawn from service in August and scrapped in December 1948. Always a 10LT8, in other words an AEC Renown chassis fitted from new with a type A165 oil engine and carrying a 60 seat LGOC built "Bluebird" body, in this case numbered 13419, it gave long service in east London, chiefly from Barking garage.

CR32 was garaged at Chalk Farm for two years commencing in January 1947 and sometime in April 1948 it was photographed helping out on Route 68. It is seen heading south along Kingsway while on a journey to West Norwood in lovely springtime weather conditions. This small capacity bus first entered service in November 1939 operating from Uxbridge garage. It received an overhaul in March 1942 soon after which it was placed in store until reappearing in June 1946 from Putney Bridge garage. Its comparatively short operational life came to an end when in May 1949 it was withdrawn from service. (V.C.Jones)

Someone has managed to catch their bus at Peckham Rye in the time honoured tradition of hopping on at the traffic lights. In this case LT471 while engaged on Route 12 and making its way to Dulwich Library, a terminus known nowadays as Dulwich, The Plough. Behind another member of the class follows on Route 63 while a further LT waits at the stop where Nunhead crews habitually changed buses. (W.J.Haynes)

By 1948 the 7T7 class, originally Green Line coaches and later Country Area buses, were pressed into use at more or less any garage who experienced a shortage of single deck buses. Here Croydon garage are utilising T230 on their 234A route between Wallington and Old Lodge Lane at Purley. This was to be the last allocation of the bus before it was withdrawn and dismantled in December 1948. (Vanguard Bus Prints)

Until fairly recently fairgrounds provided much to interest the bus enthusiast with the many former buses and coaches being re-used. On 17th May 1948 much altered ex-General S892 provides living accommodation for fairground staff or owners. The vehicle when first built was one of a number of 30 seat single deck S type fitted with solid tyres and it was initially allocated to Athol Street garage in October 1923. It survived in service long enough to carry London Transport livery and finished its days in London passenger service at Harrow Weald garage on Route 230. Here, forty five years old, proudly carrying its original operator's logo on the radiator and fitted with pneumatic tyres which had replaced the solid type while it was in service with General, it vividly reminds one of the unwitting attractions of the fair coming to town. (A.B.Cross)

Seen having just left the old Glasgow Paddocks Bus Station in Doncaster on 25th March 1948 in "as bought" condition, ex-Q4 has a few years further service to complete as a bus with G.H.Ennifer Ltd., who traded as Blue Ensign. The operator's name is not carried except in the legal owner's details, although the vehicle first entered service with them on 23rd July 1947. Originally this experimental double deck AEC Q chassis with Weymann central entrance 56 seat bodywork carried the normal three piece blind box favoured by London Transport but the route number and via points apertures have been covered over. The lower front of the vehicle is now fitted with an imitation AEC radiator grille although the lighting arrangement is still in situ. The cloth capped gentleman sitting next to the driver is George Ennifer himself who at this date had little to do with the running of the firm but put his hand in at some driving when called upon. (R.Holmes)

The bodywork fitters at Sutton garage have been told to wait since LT1071 was needed to keep the 213 service going on the 22nd October 1948. Even the route blind looks to have been fitted in a hurry and so the photographer caught the "scooter" in a rather patchy state at the Fountain Hotel in New Malden on its way to Belmont. Close examination of the seated passengers reveals that the perimeter seating is still in use. This was first fitted in February 1942 to allow a maximum of 20 standing passengers to aid wartime transport. This particular bus was to see out its operational life without being re-converted to the normal layout. The bus, a 1LTL1 carrying body number 10336, was withdrawn from service in August 1949 and despatched to R.L.Daniels. (A.B.Cross)

The story of Route 147 is related in the caption to a photograph in the 1946 section of this book. At the time the route was re-extended to Redbridge Station in May 1948, Forest Gate garage took over the Saturday and Sunday allocation from Seven Kings. Here their STL2067 waits at Redbridge Station before commencing the short journey to Ilford Station via The Drive. The bus is a combination of a 1937 built chassis to which is now mounted an LPTB 1939 manufactured body originally carried by STL2537. The practically all red livery indicates the body had been overhauled in the short period between November 1945 and May 1946 when this style was being applied. (R.Burrell)

G266 was delivered to the LPTB on 11th May 1945 and first entered service on 1st August from Victoria garage in a livery of two shades of brown. In September 1948 it received the more appropriate livery associated with Central Area bus operation and here it stands alongside Enfield garage which has been its home since November 1945. It is ready for another trip on the irregular Route 121 to Chingford, which in 1948 could involve a lengthy wait at the Ponders End Station level crossing. Bodywork is of Massey manufacture and the complete vehicle is classified 1/3G9. (W.J.Haynes)

ST431 stands at the Chipstead Valley Road terminus at How Lane of Route 166, which was the new number introduced on 7th April 1948 for the weekday operation of Route 59. A fine example of the 1930s type of passenger shelter can be seen in the background with passengers patiently waiting for the crew to bring their vehicle off the stand and head back to Thornton Heath Pond, at that time the northern extent of the renumbered route.

A nice variety of types at Victoria Station with Leyton garage's LT261 soon to depart for Chingford on Route 38. RT166, another vehicle from the same garage, waits on the extreme left of the picture before leaving on Route 10 to Woodford Bridge. A Loughton garaged STD on Route 38A behind the LT and an STL on Route 16 from Cricklewood complete the picture taken on 19th October 1948. (A.B.Cross)

Standing outside Sutton garage are, from left to right, CR38, CR3 and CR47 which must have made the journey from nearby Merton garage as they were never officially allocated to the former. It does appear that all three have been used in service as they all carry A garage plates and running numbers 26 - 28 with CR47 still showing a route blind which suggests it has worked a short journey on the 93 route to the "Woodstock". (Vanguard Bus Prints)

CR15 was one of only six of the production examples numbered CR12b to CR17b, to enter service from Windsor garage just two months after the declaration of World War II. After a prolonged storage at the same garage for most of the war years it reappeared alongside the rest of the green batch at Streatham garage in June 1946 for relief work. It was transferred to Chalk Farm garage immediately after repaint to red in October 1948. Here it stands in Buck Street, Camden Town with the familiar ABC Bakery offices in the background. This was the new stand for Route 74 in 1949 and the Chalk Farm allocation covered the summer additional service between here and Marylebone to cope with visitors to the Zoo. (J.G.S.Smith collection)

Unique for a period of its career with London Transport, RT110 lost its front roof route box due to an incident in the war years. Here at the Empress Hall, Earls Court in post-war livery which it had received in 1946, it stands at the short working terminus on Route 74 before leaving for Camden Town. The advertisement for Morris cars has an odd slogan with overtones of propaganda added which says "Let's speed the day". (G.F.Ashwell)

Pictured in Minories, Dalston garaged LT1311 advertises the latest Cary Grant and Ann Sheridan movie "You Can't Sleep Here", the so-called prize comedy of the year. While this LT makes its way to Dulwich Library, Old Kent Road's LT190 follows on Route 42 to Camberwell Green. It is remarkable that forty six years later the same routes still cover the same roads although the buses are two shades of green and cream and maroon respectively. (J.G.S.Smith collection)

This picture might well have been included in the main 1946 section of this book at which time the 34 allocation was totally LT. However, LT920 was a "rogue" allocation to Palmers Green garage in 1949 when the new SRTs were failing and the STLs were soldiering on. Here it pauses at Arnos Grove Station on duty AD27 as it makes it way somewhat unusually to Whetstone where it will turn short in the forecourt of the Black Bull public house. (Vanguard Bus Prints)

It is presumed that this picture was taken at Cox and Danks' yard at Feltham which was where the bodies of the two LTs, 772 and 1239, were scrapped in February 1949, the chassis following a similar fate the next month. However, T311 on the left is recorded as being dismantled by the LTE themselves in March 1949 but perhaps the records are wrong. The unknown STL in the background appears to be in use as some sort of temporary office accommodation and part of a blind display has been used to ensure the privacy of the management.

ST77 makes its way along Richmond Road on the outskirts of Kingston while operating a short working on Route 65 to Hook on 20th August 1949. Entering service in April 1930 from Hammersmith garage, it originally was fitted with an ST1/1 body of the type with one piece front route indicator aperture set above the driver's cab between decks. It finished its operational life with London Transport in January 1950 carrying an ST2/1 type body number 12348 as shown. There were only ten ST bodies built with the blind box set into the driver's roof canopy and before the war a via points board would have been used, the clips for which can be seen below the lamp bracket which was mounted to illuminate the board. (D.Purcell)

Parked on the road setts at Honor Oak, LT911 garaged at Nunhead waits for its next trip to commence on Route 63 to Kings Cross. Entering service in January 1932 as a 2LT5, the bus finished operational duties with LTE in January 1950 as a 1/12LT5/8, basically the same type of vehicle with a diesel engine fitted in place of its original petrol powered version. Renovation by Mann Egerton of Norwich in 1946 probably contributed to its longevity. (F.W.Ivey)

The subject of this photograph, SRT29, is seen about to turn at a busy looking Arnos Grove Station. Also to be seen are a Mann Egerton TD single decker operating from Muswell Hill garage on Route 251 and SRT16 due to leave on Route 34 to the Crooked Billet at Walthamstow before SRT29. The chassis of STL2576 sits beneath this Park Royal body which in later years found further use as RT4450. Palmers Green's allocation of SRTs was short lived and these gleaming new vehicles were quickly relegated unofficially to peak hour duties only, the older STLs being preferred. At the end of June 1949 a test on the slope of Longmore Avenue at the northern end of Route 34 proved once and for all the inefficiency of the brakes and all vehicles were modified before further service. (S.A.Newman)

The date is 7th May 1949 and Willesden's ST652 is about to leave Victoria Station on Route 52 to Mill Hill. The following month the bus was withdrawn from service and disposed of to R.L.Daniels but visually it looks in pretty good shape. STL2058 stands alongside operating from Cricklewood garage on Route 16 and scheduled for a full run through to Sudbury Town. (R.A.O'Sullivan)

Well weathered, long time servant of Muswell Hill garage, LT1097 stands sadly neglected with a front entrance STL and other clutter associated with this yard situated on the Tilbury Road which proved to be the vehicle's resting place until eventually being scrapped. The LT is now used for the undignified purpose of a tip with an assortment of varying materials clearly seen mounting within its LGOC built body. (David Jones collection)

As with so many ex-London buses and coaches, this example, originally T196, had a most interesting existence. Entering service with a Hall Lewis 27 seat rear entrance body in September 1930 it was put to work from Bishops Stortford garage on Green Line services which had previously been operated by the Acme Pullman Services Ltd. with Gilford coaches. Before the outbreak of war this 7T7 coach along with the rest of the type was withdrawn from Green Line duties and was sold to the Arlington Motor Company in London. It was then put into service by Valliant Direct Coaches Ltd. of West London who eventually had the body replaced by a new Duple front entrance 32 seat coach body. It reached Faiers (W.G.Clarke) of Felixstowe in October 1947 and it is with this owner that it is seen in this view. Eastern Counties Omnibus Co.Ltd. purchased the business of Clarke's Services as it was then known and gave GH3818 the fleet number KS904. It was withdrawn and disposed of to Ben Jordan, the Coltishall dealer in August 1952. (D.A.Jones)

Route 243 started as Route 621 on 10th April 1929 when single deck K class vehicles were first used on this circular route. Prior to that in 1928 F.H.Bruce attempted to serve the Nunhead area with his Newlands District service which fell foul of the law. New T type single deckers were allocated by LGOC in 1930 and double deck vehicles made their appearance from 12th September 1945. Eventually the route was renumbered 173 in line with its double deck status and on 23rd January 1970 it became P3 one of the first to have double deck o-m-o operation. ST108 had a varied history having first entered service in March 1930 in Central Area livery. It completed a spell operating with a gas producer trailer between May 1943 and November 1944 and then soon after reverting to petrol it gained Country Area livery. In December 1948 it was restored to red livery and put to work from Old Kent Road garage being withdrawn in October 1949. Here it turns into Rye Lane at the King's Arms. (F.W.Ivey)

Still to be converted from petrol to diesel, LTC9 is seen at Oxford Road, Putney helping out on Route 14 with duty plates F17. Paper stickers as used on the hired coaches of the period are used for a blind. These vehicles comprised an AEC petrol powered Renown chassis to which a rather heavy looking Weymann body was mounted and all twenty four first appeared in late 1937 or early 1938. The heavy appearance of the vehicles imparted a sense of substantial quality. What a pity one was not preserved to remind us of the opulence of the thirties. (R.Wellings)

Whilst those of us of the age have fond memories of petrol engined STLs, Route 65 was also associated with the ST class for a considerable number of years and red liveried ST764 is seen in 1949 en-route for Chessington Zoo with running plates V52. Before the year had ended the bus had left the capital for the scrapping fields of R.L.Daniels over in Rainham. (F.W.Ivey)

Within days of being withdrawn from passenger service in September 1949, LT177 at Victoria appears to be confused as to the exact route it is operating and how far it is going. The route is the 38 and it is likely that Chingford will be the ultimate destination. This was the LT which ran for several years from Elmers End garage using only the strip blind in the cab roof. It can be seen in this condition on page 131 of the 1948 book of this series. Obviously Leyton garage have repaired the main blind but are having problems with the strip blind. By this sad era of its life this LT carried body number 12842 and was classified as a 1/12LT5/5. (D.A.Jones)

Running along Westbury Avenue, green liveried ST1085 works from Enfield garage during its last month of service with LTE. Route 144B from Alexandra Park to Forty Hill originated in the revision of services on the Great Cambridge Road in February 1938 and continued unaltered until renumbered 231 in May 1954. This Ransome, Sims and Jefferies 2/1ST9 first entered service in June 1930 in the Autocar fleet as their number 130, passing to LGOC for operation by East Surrey in November 1930. It finished its operational duties in April 1949 and its body was immediately scrapped, its chassis suffering a similar fate the following month. (David Jones collection)

Q12, a Leatherhead based bus but here working from Addlestone garage, picks up some passengers in the rain as it journeys to Addlestone working as a relief on Green Line route 717. (P.J.Marshall)

This broadside view of STL974 taken on 25th April 1949 carrying an LPTB front entrance body, number 14830, is included here to show the arrangement of the platform area and rearward facing staircase of an STL6 sub-class body. The view was originally taken to display the available commercial advertising space on this type of Country Area vehicle but it also gives the viewer the chance to study the poor asymmetric region below the vehicle's lower length. The streamlined wheel arch assemblies come to an abrupt end and are continued by a very narrow life guard. In the opinion of the author a wider one would have carried the line to a much more satisfactory and pleasing finish. The interior colour scheme, which changes halfway up the window height, is easily visible as is also the position of the fare stage table and the single step into the lower saloon from the narrow platform. (LT Museum U46741)

As shown by the board below the nearside rear window, LT1086 was used as the R.L.Daniels canteen at Rainham. The blocked off front entrance has the inscription "Cosy Cafes" added while the way in is through the original emergency doorway which could be shut when the wind blew up off the Rainham marshes. From November 1943 until its withdrawal in April 1949 the bus had been allocated to Tottenham working the 236 route from Leyton to Finsbury Park and Stroud Green.

In 1942 the "unfrozen" batch of eleven STD class Leyland TD7 chassis with Park Royal bodywork entered service on Route 10 from Victoria garage replacing STL vehicles which were this garage's contribution to the route. STD111 is pictured at Victoria about to depart for Woodford Bridge. The chassis of this batch were very similar to the pre-war TD4 model and were powered by the Leyland 8.6 litre direct injection oil engine. Austerity type bodywork was fitted being wood framed, deficient in curves and fitted with 56 seats finished in leather. A metal panel was fitted in place of the normal glazed upper deck rear emergency exit but this was subsequently glazed as this 1949 view shows. In 1951 the entire batch was withdrawn from service after continued complaints from garage staff and passengers after which they were used as staff buses or training vehicles before being disposed of between 1953 and 1955.

Victoria garaged SRT61 has strayed on to Route 77A from its intended use on Route 10 in this photograph of the vehicle taken at the south end of Lambeth Bridge. The bus, using the chassis of former STL2637, first entered service in June 1949 and was destined not to reside at GM for many months. During the first week of September all Victoria's SRTs were moved to Cricklewood garage for use on Route 16 as part of the policy to restrict this unpopular type for use on routes more suited to their underpowered engines. (R.F.Mack)

The Docks were a natural target for the Luftwaffe in the Second World War and on 15th January 1941 a rail replacement service on the old Gallions branch was introduced for the Port of London Authority between Custom House and Manor Way. The route ran from the south side of Custom House Station between the railway line and Royal Victoria Dock until Connaught Road where it ran out of P.L.A. premises for about 50 yards. It then entered Royal Albert Dock enclosure and ran parallel to the Dock just north of it to Royal Albert Dock No.5 Shed near Manor Way and adjacent to Route 101. The journey time was 9 minutes. Here, Athol Street's STL587 is seen on the service which had remarkable longevity, lasting until early May 1969, at which time it passed to a private coach operator. At various times it was in the hands of C, CL and latterly PR and BW who used RTLs. This STL ended its days as a recruiting office at Peckham garage in 1953 after which it was exported to the Canary Isles. (L.Housden collection)

One hopes the woman striding purposefully across Victoria bus station didn't walk straight into the photographer who had his eyes on a part of history which would be lost forever when LT1262 was withdrawn from service in February 1950. A replacement piece of glass has been fitted to the front indicator but as yet the usual masking has not been applied making it difficult to set the blind neatly. The LGOC influence in the stops and lamps is still evident and also in the view are an STL on Route 25B and a post-war STD on Route 38A. (R.A.O'Sullivan)

Between October 1948 and May 1949 diminutive CR30 was garaged at Hornchurch and in this photograph operates as RD1 on Route 238 which ran between Emerson Park and Noak Hill. Although the bus has had a nasty little knock on the front panel this does not appear to interfere with its operation, a benefit of having a rear engine. The 238 was one of the few remaining o-m-o routes in the Central Area after the war and was converted to conductor operation using Ts on 20th July 1949. (A.B.Cross)

LT1199, garaged at Elmers End, is seen at the Crooked Billet, Penge on 22nd April 1950 with stable mate LT1101 parked further along the road. The lead vehicle although not being rebuilt by Marshalls was fitted with an oil engine in July 1950 and would eventually be withdrawn from service in November 1952 having completed nearly twenty two years of service to Londoners. (D.Purcell)

A large number of the vehicles garaged at Kingston are lined up alongside the railway in Gordon Road in this very interesting view taken in September 1950 and includes vehicles of Q, T, TD and RT classes. Q13 still wears its Country Area livery while the vehicle of the same class parked in front has received a repaint into the latest Central Area colour scheme and further along the line up a mixture of old and new liveried buses can be observed. Just one lucky black cat poses for the camera with no other road vehicles or people to spoil this vista of twenty vehicles. (N.S.Aston)

This picture, taken at South Croydon on 3rd June 1950, proves how erroneous information can be manufactured in a photograph. The 133 route never went any further south than the Red Deer at South Croydon and yet the blind appears genuinely set for a trip to Caterham Valley. In fact the destination belongs to the next display down which is for Route 197. LPTB bodied STL1325 entered service from Hackney garage in May 1936 as a 3/9STL11 carrying body number 16313. With just six months further passenger service before withdrawal, it now has an STL12 type body, number 17919, two years younger than the chassis. (D.Purcell)

Another ST bus to initially escape the scrap merchant's torches was ST346, which is seen here in Doncaster on 3rd May 1950 whilst in the ownership of the Ballet Montmartre, a name which seems a little out of place in these solid Yorkshire surroundings. The bus had originally been disposed of to R.L.Daniels in August 1949 for scrap but was sold on for use in this new transport role. (A.B.Cross)

Shiny looking T34 rests at the Staines West Station terminus of Route 218 on 24th June 1950 before returning to Kingston, its home base, on duty K18. This is one of two 1T1s which, at some stage in their careers, were fitted with rounded cabs similar to the single deck LTs. T34 received this modification in April 1942. The bus would eventually complete its service career with London Transport just over two years after this picture was taken. (D.Purcell)

Looking south on Chertsey Lane, Staines on 17th June 1950, ST140 approaches under the lowbridge with a headroom of 13'8" which necessitated the use of such vehicles and indeed prolonged their active life. This ST first entered service with National in May 1930 being later absorbed into the London General Country Services and then the Country Area of LPTB. In August 1941 it received Central Area red livery only to regain its more traditional colours in November 1944. It was withdrawn from service in October 1952 and later served with J.W.H.Watson (Wilberjim Coaches) of Strood before passing on to A.E.Moore of Romford, eventually to be scrapped in 1954. (J.C.Gillham)

The last remnants of ex-LT1081 stand somewhere near a railway line in the summer of 1950. The flat body now fitted gives a good insight into the height and arrangement of the chassis beneath. The fuel tank is still mounted to the chassis as in LT days although the rear tyres look as if they are more suited for use over rough terrain than for use on the streets of the capital. The cab and its roof have been retained giving a rather unbalanced finish to the final product. (L.Housden collection)

Harrow Weald garage was the last to receive an allocation of the new SRT class and these entered service in January 1950 on Route 114 running between Edgware and Rayners Lane Station. The full complement of buses for this route was twenty two but with only sixteen new vehicles and a few drafted in from other garages the service was never wholly maintained by the class and a few STLs remained in use alongside these hybrids. SRT150, whose Park Royal body sits on the chassis of former STL2361, is seen at Rayners Lane. By October the SRTs at HD had been replaced by RTW class vehicles which themselves were replaced by RTs in the following April.
(Lens of Sutton)

Front entrance STL1021 stands at the Staines Central Station terminus of Route 441 on 2nd July 1950 with blinds which need a little adjustment for its return journey. Built with an LPTB 48 seat body and, in line with the rest of the batch, the seating was increased, in this instance in August 1939, by the fitting of four extra seats over the wheel arches. Just a little over twelve years later the original body was exchanged for this Weymann built example and this combination was to continue in service until the bus was withdrawn in November 1950. (D.Purcell)

Due to roadworks in the Strand which lasted nearly a month, a diversion was put into operation for eastbound buses via Victoria Embankment. STD70 is seen in Temple Place at the junction of Surrey Street on 10th August 1950, four days before normal working was restored. Less than two months later this piece of road would receive its own permanent bus route in the form of northbound buses on the first of the Kingsway Subway tram replacement routes, the 170. (L.Housden collection)

This unusual front view of C59 while it awaits further duty from Dorking garage on 9th July 1950 prompts the question why wasn't a bumper fitted? The Short Bros. bodies, of which this is one, were normally fitted with them whereas the Weymann bodied versions did not carry them. Maybe the bumper had fallen off having fulfilled its intended purpose of protection! (D.Purcell)

Standing in Queen Victoria Road, High Wycombe on 3rd June 1950, "unfrozen" STL2681 from the 17STL batch is about to work to Penn Post Office although the route number is incorrectly set. It should be showing 362B. The mismatch between the front mudguards is explained by standard AEC examples being in place when the chassis was delivered to Chiswick while the differing bodies attached to the chassis in 1942 had one already in place which was appropriate to the body. The bus was later used as a staff bus in the Central Area until eventually being disposed of to Norths, the well known dealer, in January 1956. (D.Purcell)

STL490 carries a similar body to that with which it first entered service in London way back in July 1934. Now nearing the end of its revenue earning capacity it is seen passing a fine line up of taxis on 26th July 1951 as it makes its way from the Golders Green bus station heading for Cricklewood Broadway by way of Route 226. Double deck buses took over operation of this route from single deck Q type on 14th December 1949. (G.F.Ashwell)

Seen in Doncaster near to Waterdale with another of G.H.Ennifer's vehicles, a Crossley FDT202, just behind, much altered ex-Q4 still journeys to Rossington as in the picture in the 1948 section of this supplement. An oil engine is now carried in place of the original petrol version and the front of the vehicle now carries decorative strips having been rebuilt by H.Hartley and Co. whose advertisement appears on the front panel. Other than these alterations the 3Q3 type bus appears to be basically in the condition in which it pursued its short career as a Country Area service bus in 1940. (R.Holmes)

The playwright George Bernard Shaw died in 1950 and the house at Ayot St.Lawrence, aptly named "Shaw's Corner", where he had lived for forty four years, passed to the National Trust and became a tourist attraction. On 24th March 1951 Country Buses introduced Route 315 on Wednesdays to Sundays between Welwyn Garden City and Wheathampstead to cater for the expected visitors. The panel timetable even showed the times of connecting trains from London at Welwyn Garden City. Hatfield were allocated a Leyland Cub for the route and here C23 waits in Welwyn Garden City before departing on one of the short workings to Shaw's Corner. The route ceased operation after 12th August never to return. Further down the road RT1088 is working the 340 route via Barnet By Pass to Potters Bar and New Barnet. (R.K.Blencowe)

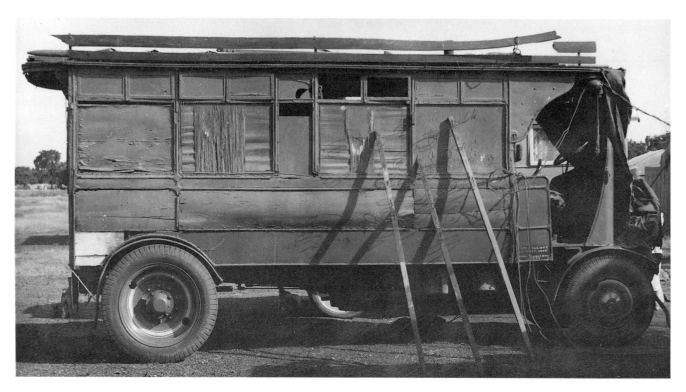

Some help is needed in identifying this relic from the past. The photograph was taken at Wanstead Flats on 3rd August 1951 and although the note on the reverse of the print says "LGOC NS XR739", this combination cannot be found in any records available. NS650 was registered XP739 so possibly this is what is meant although there are many features on this body which do not tie up with an NS. Any information about this picture will be gratefully received. (John H.Meredith)

On weekend loan from Cricklewood to Watford High Street garage, SRT50 is seen passing through Watford while making its way to Maple Cross on Route 351 on rostered duty WA38. The chassis used for this hybrid bus once belonged to STL2617, a 15STL16 with LPTB built body number 196 dating from 1939. The STL ended its passenger carrying career operating from Dunton Green garage in November 1948 to re-emerge in the summer of 1949 suitably modified as an 8RT9 and carrying a Park Royal body numbered 4657 in the LT series. In October 1953 it was withdrawn from service, the chassis being scrapped and the body remounted on to new RT4404 to again be allocated to Cricklewood garage. The advertisements are intriguing and one feels the children might prefer going to the Bertram Mills Circus rather than being taken to Harrods. All a case of proper upbringing I suppose! (A.B.Cross)

In 1951 ex-T251 was operated by a coach concern by the name of S.G.Norris. This AEC Regal with front entrance coach body had first entered service from Hitchin garage in January 1931. The bodywork is basically in the condition as built although embellishments and minor alterations have been made. The destination box is reduced in height, a driver's door has been added and fancy panelling is fitted to the front of the saloon doorway. Towards the end of the year the vehicle moved on to the dealer, Deacon of Dorchester and it must be presumed was then scrapped, no further sightings of this twenty year old coach being reported.

An interesting view in more ways than one as G347 sits beneath the trolleybus wiring for the 693/695 terminus at Wangey Road, Chadwell Heath together with G332 carrying identical bodywork. The driver of the lead vehicle heaves himself into his cab before setting out for Upminster Station on the 86A route. The section of this route between here and Upminster was the most intensive at the time, less than half the buses making the full journey from Limehouse. Route 86A lost its suffix in the changes which accompanied the replacement of the Chadwell Heath Trolleybus routes in 1959 and after several changes still exists today although only running between Stratford and Romford. The cinema advertising on specially shaped billboards tells us that "Midnight Episode" and "Sirocco" are showing at the Whalebone Lane Odeon while alternatively "Bright Leaf" and "This Side of the Law" can be seen at the Green Lane Odeon. (A.B. Cross)

This picture illustrates the use in 1952 of both the original Amersham & District buildings and the 1935 garage built at Amersham by the LPTB. C18 stands outside and a 10T10 is parked within the older structure while various buses can be seen in the newer premises. Ironically parts of the old buildings still remain today while a Tesco supermarket and petrol station have replaced the newer structure. (J.G.S.Smith collection)

Photographed on 30th April 1952 and in company with a Bedford service vehicle, this 5 ton tower wagon, 733J, has an interesting ancestry. The chassis and front portion of the lower deck of its LGOC double deck body came from STL9 which had been withdrawn from service in April 1948 and which, at the time, carried body number 13498 of STL1 classification. The tower structure had previously been mounted on a much earlier solid tyred ADC '418' chassis numbered 10E in the service vehicle fleet. This had previously carried the number 123 until 1939 when the remaining vehicles which had been taken over in the 1933 formation of LPTB were renumbered into a common system. (L.Housden collection)

RF39 has been shown before in this series of books but this print is included for the fine evocative view it gives of New Cross Gate in the final days of the trams and the first days of RF operation on Green Line services. It is also long before the one-way traffic scheme at this point under which the coach could no longer turn direct into New Cross Road as it does here. (L.Housden collection)

STL1763, with a full complement of route blinds, albeit a side rather than front intermediate point blind, stands at the bus and coach stop outside Amersham garage while working Route 353 to Berkhamsted Station. The date is 3rd June 1952, just twelve months prior to the bus being withdrawn from passenger service use. Before reaching the end of its career it would be further transferred to Two Waters, Garston and finally Watford High Street garages. The bus is a 4/9STL14 and the LPTB built body carries number 17126, originally mounted on the chassis of STL1840. (Lyndon Rowe)

Used as a terminus since the days of the B type, Plumstead Common provides the resting place for a number of RT family buses. The lead vehicle is Plumstead's RTL591 still wearing the earlier colour scheme and restricted blind arrangement for its use on Route 53. Other RTs further along the road wear the latest paint scheme with a full complement of blinds for their involvement on Route 163. (A.Mortimer)

Ex-T277 is now someone's permanent residence at Chevening Halt, Dunton Green in use as a "mobile home". In the 1949 book of this series the same vehicle is seen going about its duties in the capital. Disposed of to R.L.Daniels in May 1950 it finally found use in this role and lasted until it was burnt on site in 1969. Despite the addition of a chimney, an individualistic paint scheme and added protection for the wheels it still shows its unmistakable Green Line pedigree. (F.W.Ivey)

Standing in Guildhouse Street alongside Victoria garage, Saunders bodied RT1396 shows signs of its three years of service within the capital and still carries restricted route blinds which are set for service on Route 52. The two advertisers appear to complement each other, which presumably is just a coincidence. (Museum of London)

P.A.Y.E. RF700 in Epsom town centre operates Route 419 between Epsom, Brettgrave and Langley Vale, a large development in the vicinity of the famous racecourse. Route 419 operated by Leatherhead garage was the first route chosen for one-man operation by full size single deckers using three RF class vehicles with seating well in excess of the then regulatory 26 for this type of operation. The three buses entered service in March 1954 and worked the route for a little over four months after which the experiment was continued by Two Waters garage using Route 316 as the guinea pig. In the spring of 1955 this RF could once again be seen on Route 419. (A.Mortimer)

Overhauled the previous year, Craven bodied RT1437 looks in smart condition with its new paint scheme and full set of route blinds. It is parked here on a wet and dismal day alongside Croydon garage. (A.Mortimer)

Putney Bridge garage's RT88 picks up passengers in London Road, Morden before continuing its journey to Epsom Station on Route 93. Although there are a number of people in the photograph and a good potential load for the bus there is a distinct lack of other road vehicles in this view taken in November 1954. A present day photographer would find this an impossible shot in the traffic conditions today. (A.Mortimer)

RT2951 stands beside Sutton garage ready for use on duty A41 on Route 164A which operated between Tattenham Corner Station and Morden. This RT had first entered service in November 1952 from Merton garage and carries a Park Royal RT8/2 body. When RT1 was revealed to the public before the war it oddly carried blinds for this route but it was many years before the AEC Regents actually found their way on to it. (A.Mortimer)

The Upton Park practice of placing the fleet number on the rear dome and the registration DGX322 confirms the identity of STL2020. It is one of two STLs seen in some sort of dealer's yard situated in the Belgian capital of Brussels. It is reported that the vehicles - the other being STL703 - were en-route for Yugoslavia but had broken down and found temporary accommodation on this site. Whether they were sold on the spot is not known but by the time this photograph was taken the dealer appears to be offering STL2020 for the bargain price of 16,000 Belgian Francs.

In 1954 Upton Park garage operated both Leyland and AEC members of the RT family and RTL8 and RT333 are seen on Route 175. The RTL is blinded for a garage journey while the RT is destined East Ham, Manor Way, from which point buses often worked dead to the garage. Both buses have received overhauls since first entry into service in 1948 and the picture emphasises the differences between the early RT3 body carried by the RT and the later type of body on the RTL. Note also the different styles of intermediate point blind for the same route. (A.Mortimer)

What at one time might have been described as "a fine detached residence" in the shape of ex-T297 was first noted as Luton, Chatham in March 1950 having only been disposed of to R. L. Daniels the previous month. By 1954 the bus was looking past its prime but still managed to provide interest to lovers of London Transport vehicles until it was scrapped on site in 1961 having nearly reached its thirtieth year of existence. See the 1949 book of this series for two views of the bus in happier times when it was working the 458 route from Slough to Uxbridge.

An interesting view of STL2171 as it stands in Crawley Old Town. It awaits departure on Route 483 which operated between here and Northgate, a then newly developed neighbourhood a mile or so to the north of the town centre. This particular bus started life in September 1937 as a 4/9STL15 carrying a Park Royal metal framed body numbered 17592. In May 1949, at its final body change, a composite LPTB built body of STL16 type, numbered 98 originally carried by STL2573, eliminated the metal framed body then fitted. After its disposal it appeared as a full fronted van with Entwhistle Transport based at Wigan. (R.Wellings)

BLH875, alias STL1034, is definetly not going anywhere just now in this view taken at the Denver Chemical Company's premises at Rainham. Once a front entrance Country Area bus, the chassis and cab later saw service as a drop-sided lorry, No. 50 in the Denver fleet. In its operational years with London Transport, which stretched from May 1935 to April 1951, the body and chassis stayed matched throughout its various visits to Chiswick overhaul works. In its latter years it has obtained an AEC radiator badge in place of the London Transport one it carried in service and despite its dire straits it still clings to this link with its origins.

In the book of this series covering the year 1952 the much decayed body of LT494, which was once mounted on this chassis, can be viewed in use as a chicken house. On 18th September 1955 the chassis is seen at the same Ferny Hill Farm near Cockfosters fitted out as a lorry. This LT bus entered service in June 1931 being withdrawn from service by LTE in August 1949 and was originally disposed of to R.L.Daniels in the same month. (N.Rayfield)

APPENDIX I

London Transport Central and Country Area Bus Garages

A	Sutton	HN*	Hitchin
AB	Twickenham	HW	Hanwell
AC	Willesden	J	Holloway
AD	Palmers Green	K	Kingston
AE	Hendon	L	Loughton
AF	Chelverton Road, Putney	LH*	Leatherhead
AH	Nunhead	LS*	Luton
AK	Streatham	M	Mortlake
AL	Merton	MA*	Amersham
AM	Plumstead	MH	Muswell Hill
AP	Seven Kings	N	Norwood
AR	Tottenham	NF*	Northfleet
AV	Hounslow	ON	Alperton
B	Battersea	P	Old Kent Road
BK	Barking	PB	Potters Bar
C	Athol Street, Poplar	Q	Camberwell
CF	Chalk Farm	R	Hammersmith
CL	Clay Hall	RD	Hornchurch
CM*	Chelsham	RE*	London Road, Romford
CS	Chiswick (non-operational)	RG*	Reigate
CY*	Crawley	S	Shepherds Bush
D	Dalston	SA*	St Albans
DG*	Dunton Green	SJ*	Swanley Junction
DS*	Dorking	SP	Sidcup
DT*	Dartford	ST*	Staines
E	Enfield	T	Leyton
ED	Elmers End	TB	Bromley
EG*	East Grinstead	TC	Croydon
EP*	Epping	TG*	Tring
EW	Edgware	TL	Catford
F	Putney Bridge	TW*	Tunbridge Wells
G	Forest Gate	U	Upton Park
GD*	Godstone	UX	Uxbridge
GF*	Guildford	V	Turnham Green
GM	Gillingham Street, Victoria	W	Cricklewood
GY*	Grays	WA*	Watford High Street
H	Hackney	WG	West Green
HD	Harrow Weald	WR*	Windsor
HE*	High Wycombe	WT*	Leavesden Road, Watford
HF*	Hatfield	WY*	Addlestone
HG*	Hertford	X	Middle Row
HH*	Two Waters, Hemel Hempstead		
		* indicates a Country Area garage.	

The above list is of all operational motorbus garages available in 1946. RE and TW had been used for other purposes during the Second World War and came back into operational use with the introduction of Green Line services early in 1946. Both these garages only operated Green Line coach routes.

APPENDIX II

A special thank you is extended to the following correspondents for their interest shown in updating or correcting information given in earlier titles in this series of books. They are: Tony Beard of 'The 2RT2 Preservation Society', Ray Corley, Peter Gomm of 'The RT1 Group', Phillip Groves, John Hillman, P. Hotchin, Barry Maynard-Smith, George Moon of 'The London Trolleybus Preservation Society', Lewis Norris and James Stirling of 'Allsorts'.

1939-45

Frontispiece	This dramatic view is taken at the corner of St. John's Hill and Plough Terrace, Battersea. The "Surrey Hounds" was never rebuilt and in its place today stands a corner wine merchants together with a low three-storey block of flats leading towards Clapham Junction in the distance.
Page 19	Q208c is parked at St. Thomas' Hospital, Westminster.
Page 19	It is confirmed that T499c together with a sister T are parked beside Hendon garage as surmised.
Page 20	T599 and an STL further along the road are parked on the east side of Cavendish Square.
Page 22	Manchester Corporation Transport 575 was photographed in Margaret Street, just off Oxford Circus.
Page 39	The upper picture was taken at Ide Hill and T651 stands immediately outside 'Rosemary Cottage'. Just out of view at the right of the picture stands the 'Cock Inn'.
Page 47	The east side of Cavendish Square is the resting place of STL1150.
Page 56	This picture of RT1 is one of a series taken at the 'Spaniards Inn', Hampstead Heath on 13th July 1939.
Page 57	Other notable differences between the prototype and production examples of the "pre-war" RTs consisted of the front dome which was set further forward on RT1, being mounted with a somewhat squatter roof number box. Window handles were centrally placed whereas on the production batch they were fitted towards the outer edges of the windows.
Page 62	STL1046 is pictured at Bletchingley, a village which lies on the main A25 between Redhill and Godstone.
Page 64	The upper photograph shows T596 resting in Little Missenden.
Page 65	The American Red Cross offices on the corner of Denmark Street are in fact the famous "Rainbow Club", primarily for use by personnel serving in the armed forces.
Page 66	It is confirmed that the location is Barking Road by Tunmarsh Lane at the 'Greengate'.
Page 72	LT1210 is seen standing near the junction of Harwood Road and Tyrawley Road, south of Fulham Broadway.
Page 82	RT24 is pictured in Esher High Street, the building in the background previously having been in use as a bank.
Page 101	There are conflicting reports on the body condition of RT97 when it returned to London from Birmingham City Transport and further research is continuing.
Page 108	The lower picture depicts LTC2c and LTC5c parked in Harmood Street near Chalk Farm garage.
Page 109	These vehicles are also in the vicinity of Chalk Farm garage.
Page 114	ST733 is seen at Peckham Rye.
Page 118	The location of the lower photograph is Clapham Common.

Page 127	RT1 is depicted as it traverses the A214 at Central Hill in Upper Norwood on Good Friday 1943. The reference to cream surrounds to the windows should of course read broken white.
Page 133	The livery worn by RT19 is green, having been repainted at Chiswick Works prior to its demonstration tour. Careful inspection of the second window in the lower saloon reveals the inscription "Regent RT Bus" beneath an AEC triangle.
Page 140	Q120 is in the vicinity of the 'Lord Hill' public house at Peckham and not in the vicinity of Old Kent Road garage.
Page 142	T232 is seen at Ealing Broadway Station.
Page 147	STL2222 was photographed while making its way round Aldwych.
Page 155	The lower picture depicts loaned RV1145 travelling in the opposite direction to that stated in the caption, i.e. northbound in Whitehall.
Page 157	TF2c is parked in Abingdon Street, SW1 next to the Victoria Tower Gardens.

1948 BOOK

Page 66	STL2231 was photographed in Station Road, Harrow.
Page 138	G90 is about to turn into Forty Lane from Tudor Gardens, Kingsbury, a point known as Blackbird Cross for many years.

1949 BOOK

Page 73	T314 is pictured in Bunns Lane, Mill Hill near the junction with Page Street.

1950 BOOK

Page 19	RT1158 was photographed in Field End Road, Eastcote near Eastcote Station.

1952 BOOK

Page 121	In answer to the query posed in the caption of the lower picture there was no problem at Oxted for through traffic using the A25, passing as it does under the railway viaduct at Ravenswood. The need for lowbridge vehicles arose from the fact that the rail bridge immediately north of Oxted Station lacked clearance for highbridge vehicles. The RTL therefore would have worked light using the main arterial road to take up duties working between Westerham, Biggin Hill and Bromley. When RTs replaced RLHs on Route 410 in the early 60s, a route detour was introduced until the roadway under the offending bridge was lowered and the route resumed its normal roads.

1955 BOOK

Page 22	My reference to RT1 being owned by Peter Gomm has proved incorrect. It is in fact owned by the 'RT1 Group' and I offer my apologies to the members.
Page 62	The rather out of place 'mansion' in the background of the lower picture is a public house named 'The Swan' and is situated just up the hill from Edenbridge Station. The bus will traverse the quaintly named Troy Town before making a return journey to Horsham.
Page 90	The main function of the drop down side flap to the upper deck of tree lopper 971J was to allow the crew better and easier access to the branches of the offending trees although it was handy for sweeping out the debris at the end of the day. This picture should be credited to F.W. Ivey.
Page 120	This photograph is also from the camera of F.W. Ivey.